Really?
I Had A Stroke?

A STORY OF STROKE
AND THE BEST STRATEGIES
FOR MAXIMUM BRAIN RECOVERY

WILLIAM J. TIPPETT

TIPPETT WORKS
wjtippettbooks

Published by TIPPETT WORKS, Toronto, ON
wjtippettbooks@gmail.com

ISBN: 978-1-9991089-0-8

Editor: Donna L. Dawson, CPE
BOOK COVER DESIGN BY EBOOKLAUNCH.COM

Dedication

To all the individuals and their families who have been touched by a stroke.

And to my wife, who makes all this possible...

ABOUT THE AUTHOR

William J. Tippett, PhD, is a former assistant professor from the University of Northern British Columbia, where he was the founder and director of the Brain Research Unit (BRU). The BRU focused on elements of neuroscience including hands-on clinical investigations such as how cognitive training can positively alter the effects of stroke-related deficits and individuals diagnosed with probable Alzheimer's disease.

Dr. Tippett has held an associate membership with Centre for Stroke Recovery, which began while he worked as a post-doctoral fellow in the cognitive neurology unit at Sunnybrook Health Sciences Centre, Toronto, ON. He is an active writer and researcher examining how cognitive stimulation programs can alter the course of an illness for individuals experiencing dementia-related disturbances and stroke-related injury. He has presented at the Society for Neuroscience conference, the Centre for Stroke Recovery conference, British Columbia's Annual Psychogeriatric conference, and the Alzheimer's Association International Conference. He continues to advocate for care and advancements in the field of stroke, Alzheimer's disease and healthy cognitive aging.

Dr. Tippett is the author of *Building an Ageless Mind: Preventing and Fighting Brain Aging and Disease.*

i

PREFACE

The characters in this book are fictional; however, the strokes they experience and the symptoms, onset, diagnoses, treatment, and care are based on evidence-based research. The information in this story attempts to adhere to commonly expected outcomes, both positive and negative, that can result from one's lifestyle, timely access to treatment, and previous medical conditions and history. The stroke recovery program described in the story is also fictional but it encompasses the author's belief in a "utopia" program, based on current evidence-based research, that could significantly alter the recovery of people who have experienced stroke-related events as describe in this story.

CONTENTS

INTRODUCTION

I lay in the half-darkened room, the curtain pulled just slightly on an angle to allow some light in, but not enough to illuminate my old running medals hanging from a bookshelf across the room or the degrees hanging on the opposite wall. All that is clearly visible is the only picture hanging on my faded blue wall—my stylized copy of Vincent Van Gogh's *Café Terrace at Night*. I gaze at it almost every day after I wake.

The picture reminds me, taunts me, about the year I lived in Paris. Paris was a wonderful time—the nightlife, the cafés, great food, the exceptional wine at insanely cheap prices, but most importantly the good friends and good times. If I could only go there one more time and live as I had then, and not as I do now.

It is difficult for me to turn over in bed, which is why I'm often left starring at the picture. Many mornings I doze, drifting in and out of sleep, wishing I was somewhere besides this bed doing something other than looking at that same dull blue wall. I dream of my old life every day, of my old morning routine, when I would get up and go for a run. I would hit the road early, and the only sound was my footfall and my lungs willing air in and out. Early morning runs were great because I was usually alone on the road.

I felt so free on those mornings, the sun hitting my face on the way out and warming my back on the way home. The dull hum of the outside world was silenced while I hit the park trails, my pace my own, my own route, my run my own. It felt like success, achievement, and freedom, sweet sweet freedom.

Later, after a well-deserved shower, I would stop at the little coffee shop on the corner on my way to work. Some days the line would be long but I didn't mind. I would ease the wait by listening to the soft music playing in the background through the bustle of the shop; those rare peaceful moments were often the best part of my day: I was in a crowded shop and yet utterly alone with my thoughts. It's ironic that I used to wish for more of that time, just an extra hour or two for myself, and now that is exactly what I have too much of.

A little over eight months ago I had a stroke. I collapsed at home and lay on the floor for half the night before my housekeeper found me in the morning. I was told in the hospital that a portion of my brain had been without oxygen for a significant amount of time and that I had many complications as a result.

I had lost my ability to speak clearly, and I had lost some word-finding skills, meaning I know what I want to say but I can't remember the words. Sometimes I cannot get the words out when I do remember them. I also have paralysis in the right side of my body, so both my right arm and right leg are basically paralyzed—it's like carrying dead weight most days. And that's why I lie in bed most mornings waiting for my personal support worker to arrive and help me get up and get ready for the day.

This is not how I imagined my life would turn out. I certainly did not imagine that at the age of fifty-four I would have experienced an event like this. I keep turning it over in my mind and it just seems so unfair. I was... I am a good person and I always tried my best. Why did this happen to me? I keep thinking back to the start of it. The length of time I lay on the floor, without help. The wait in the hospital and the wait for a diagnosis, for treatment, and for follow-up treatments. I wonder if things could have been different.

That scenario could be the outcome for any individual experiencing a stroke-related event. The goals of this story are threefold:

- To help people understand what to expect if they have a stroke,
- To describe ways they may be able to prevent, or at the very least reduce, the effects of a stroke and avoid the outcome described above, and
- To outline a vision for an ideal post-stroke rehabilitation program.

Though the characters in this story are fictional, I have described the strokes they experience realistically in terms of symptoms before, during, and after the stroke. I've made an effort to show the typical consequences and recovery that a patient can expect based on the type of stroke they experience and on a number of different factors, which are often very individual, such as their personal characteristics, life choices, and experiences. I also describe the routine treatment one can currently expect at a "normal" hospital emergency department to highlight what course of treatment may be—or should be—followed after admission to a hospital.

This story is designed not only as a cautionary tale about the consequences of certain life choices, but also as a guide to help individuals who are seeking answers to questions such as

- What now?
- How should my stroke be managed?
- What outcomes can I expect?
- What outcomes should I be striving for?

The story is meant to help people who have had a stroke, are worried about having a stroke, or have had a friend or family member in stroke recovery to understand what they can expect and what to look for in recovery as a result of a stroke.

It is not my intention to highlight shortcomings in the world of stroke care and rehabilitation, but rather to empower individuals with information. I also want to reassure stroke patients and their families that this is not the end of the world; there are options and specific treatments you need to advocate for. Certain courses of action can be undertaken to help stroke patients recover better.

I've highlighted how and when one should advocate for a certain type of care and what effective treatment to look for when going to an emergency department with a suspected stroke. Admission personal are only as good as the information they receive, so providing as much detail as possible when you arrive at emergency is essential for rapid treatment and more importantly rapid diagnosis.

In recent years stroke-related deaths have been reduced in the Western world with the use of aggressive new post-stroke treatments. This trend has created a situation where recovery is now more the focus then the event itself, if caught early, strokes can be managed. But stroke patients still face many limitations for recovery, including access to equipment and facilities, location, finances, treatment knowledge, and access to the right treatment professionals.

Researchers and clinicians need to strive for a new vision and direction in evidence-based stroke treatments and apply that vision in an effort to bring about positive change and advancements in post-stroke rehabilitation. The goal of this story is to provide a framework for that vision, including what could be an optimal situation for treating individuals after a stroke and what excellent stroke care and rehabilitation might looked like in an ideal setting.

This book is intended to help guide and inspire individuals to create the best possible recovery program and positive outcomes for all patients, based on asking, "If we had unlimited resources, what would an optimal program look like? And what is the least we can do, given the limitations of our current resources?"

For example, as you will see, even the smallest application of any extra post-stroke treatment can be an effective way to create positive change and you don't necessarily need unlimited resources to effect change.

Though the story centers on stroke-related recovery, many of the training techniques described here could be used in other conditions in which the brain has experienced a significant injury or other traumatic change.

The rehabilitation program presented here is a vision of what could be in the world of stroke recovery and a vision of what an optimal program might look like. It is my goal to inform readers of what they can and should do to bring about change in the world of stroke recovery and care for themselves or their loved one. If we shoot for the stars maybe we will reach the moon, and that could mean a world of difference to many people.

PART I

REALLY? I HAD A STROKE?

CHAPTER 1
DECLAN MYLES

As I slowly opened my eyes, I was confused by my surroundings, I was in a railed bed and there was an IV penetrating my arm, as well as a blood pressure cuff secured around my other arm; in addition to these items I could feel a monitor attached to my finger. I had a dry mouth and an ache in my head and all my muscles felt sore. I looked around and saw that I was not alone in this room—there were three other people in beds like mine. I came to notice the white noise of equipment working away, strange hums surrounding me, the beige walls, the green curtains so often used between hospital beds, and the incessant beeping of a nearby machine. I turned my head slightly and saw the end of my IV was attached to electronic monitor on a stand. I was unsure if my IV had come to an end, maybe it had and perhaps that was why I was awake.

The clues led to the obvious conclusion: I was in a hospital. Questions rose quickly in my mind. Why was I here? What happened to me? Was I okay? Was I going to be okay?

I hesitated to call for a nurse right away; instead, I took a few moments to examine my surroundings a bit more and get my bearings. The other patients appeared to be sleeping. There was a woman to my right and two men on the other side of the room, separated from each other by a slight pull of a green curtain. There were very few personal items in the room, and it appeared that our clothes and other effects had been placed in clear plastic bags. These bags were on chairs next to us and were labeled, I gathered, with our names. I thought this was very orderly and my best macabre guess was that they did this in case our next stop was the morgue. I couldn't see a clock, but the light from the window had a pinkish hue to it, suggesting to me that it was likely late afternoon.

Each patient had an IV attached to them and I realized that the one that was beeping incessantly belonged to the woman to my right. The woman, if I had to guess, was about fifty-five. Strands of black hair were coming out from beneath the bandage on her head. Her face was quite tanned and looked tired, like she had experienced a lifetime of hard living by the age of forty and was fifteen years into her next lifetime of hard living. Despite this she appeared to be sleeping peacefully, as if she had not had a good night's sleep in some time. I almost envied her because I wasn't sure I had had a good sleep in a long time either.

The two other patients were very different looking men. The first was a heavy-set man, possibly in his late sixties or early seventies, with a head of thick gray hair. The other, directly across from me, was thin and had a full grayish-brown beard. Even though he was in a deep sleep, or possibly a coma for all I knew, his face had a look of great concentration, as if he were solving a complicated math problem or working out the meaning of life. If I had to guess, I'd say he appeared to be in his mid-seventies. It was hard to tell what kind of shape he was in because he was lying in a bed, but my guess was that he was fit. He was covered by a homemade quilt, suggesting that someone was taking measures to ensure his comfort, for which I envied him.

This collection of individuals offered few clues as to what I was doing here, and at the moment I was not receiving many messages from my body. What I did notice was a bit of numbness on the right side of my body, to what extent it was hard tell lying in this position. Something did not feel right; I wasn't sure but my right side didn't feel the same as the rest of my body. It was difficult to define; the feeling was just not the same. In some ways it was like pins and needles and in others it was just very numb.

I tried to move my right arm, but it would not cooperate very well. This was very strange because in my mind my intension was to move my arm; the movement should be automatic. To even think about it this much was quite alarming. I looked at my right arm and realized I just couldn't move it much. I tried the same with my left arm and was able to lift it and examine it for any damage. It looked okay to me.

I'd been a cop for the better part of thirty years, so a meticulous, pragmatic approach worked best for me. I continued to assess my left arm; it was working well, and I was relieved to discover that I could move it around, scratch my ear, do whatever I wanted. I used my left arm to pull myself up a little higher in my bed, get a little more comfortable, and have a better look around. I was very thirsty but I couldn't see any water around, so I began to search for a call button to get some assistance.

By this time my curiosity had left me and solving this mystery on my own was not something I had a great interest in at the moment, plus there was a pounding in my head that made concentrating difficult. I really needed some answers from someone who knew what was going on and why I was here. I located the small button tied to my bedrail. I had not personally spent much time in hospitals, so I guessed the button was either going to give me a good dose of medication or call a nurse. Since it appeared I had nothing to lose at this point, I pushed it repeatedly; I figured that either way it was going to be a win for me, especially with the headache.

Within moments, two nurses enter the room. This must be serious, since not only did I get a quick response, *two* nurses arrived. Maybe I was in heaven's waiting room.

"Good evening, Mr. Myles. My name is Sarah and I'm the head nurse for this ward," said the first nurse to reach me. Her badge bore that out: Sarah T., RN, Head Nurse. "You are at Lakefield General Hospital in the Integrated Stroke Research and Care Center," she explained gently.

"I'm *where*?" But nothing came out of my mouth but a jumble of words that sounded nothing like what I intended.

Sarah replied calmly, "It's okay, Mr. Myles. You're here because you had a stroke. You have been unconscious for about a day, but we're happy that you're with us. The doctor has been keeping a close watch on you. I'll page Dr. White to let her know you're awake. I'm sure you have lots of questions and she's the best one to answer them or at the very least give you some information about what happened and what brought you here. Is there anything I can get you in the meantime?"

As Sarah spoke the other nurse moved about recording readings from the various machines. She collected my blood pressure reading by pressing a button on one of the machines, after which she thankfully removed the cuff. I guess it had been on my arm for a while. I was unable to turn to read the numbers on the machine, and the nurse was no help as she gave no indication of whether the values were good or bad, which made me think, hmm... maybe nurses would make good poker players.

Before I spoke, I studied Sarah briefly; she had kind green eyes, a crooked smile, and pale white skin as if she hadn't spent more than a few minutes in the sunshine in weeks. She had long brown hair, which she had bundled up loosely at the back of her head.

I attempted to form some words, but again, not much that was understandable came out. Even though I could clearly feel I was saying "water," I could tell Sarah was struggling to understand my request. I made a drinking motion with my left arm.

"Oh, yes, of course, Mr. Myles," she responded, "I'll get you some water right away." She hurried out of the room with the other nurse and came back moments later, alone, with a small cup of ice water, with a tiny white straw. I thought, why do they always fill the cups with shaved ice, with only a dribble of water in the bottom? The nurse held the cup for me. After the smallest sip I also wonder whether the hospital was supplied exclusively with the smallest straws on Earth, perhaps as a way to save money.

The nurse brought the straw to my lips again and as I sucked on it, I realized a little water was dribbling out of the right side of my mouth. I saw now that this was going to be a frustrating process for both of us. But Sarah was very patient. She dabbed my chin and kindly said, "Don't worry, Mr. Myles. This happens to everyone. Things will get better. I'll go and page Dr. White now and I'll be back to check on you shortly."

She paused in the doorway and added reassuringly, "Don't worry, Mr. Myles. You are in good hands. This is the newest and most advanced stroke ward in the region." And with that she was off, taking quick strides in her white high-top sneakers.

After what felt like an hour, another woman appeared. I would say she was in her mid-fifties. She was dressed in a long white coat, which flowed behind her as she walked and which partially covered a long, loose-fitting plaid dress. She was wearing gold-rimmed glasses and had a face that seemed familiar, but I was certain I had never met her. She had short black hair with white streaks emerging here and there. She also had the trademark look—a stethoscope draped around her neck. I conclude that this must be Dr. White.

I was somewhat relieved. When it came to physicians, police officers, and airline pilots, people my age feel more comfortable when these individuals have a few miles on them, suggesting experience and by association knowledge.

The doctor approached my bed with determination and an air of reassurance. It was interesting that even though she had not yet spoken a word I already felt relieved she was here and looking after me. She got right to it. "Hello, I'm Evelyn White. I was the neurologist on call when you arrived yesterday afternoon. Today is Tuesday and it's about 5:50 PM. You're in Lakefield General Hospital. Your co-workers brought you here, I believe from a fire scene you were investigating. You are here because you had a stroke..." Really? I had a Stroke? is all I could think, however Dr. White continued to speak, "your fellow officers said you were in the middle of giving some instructions when your speech became slurred and your face drooped on one side. Then you went unconscious. Fortunately, you were with others when it happened and they were quick to get you here. That more than likely saved your life and, hopefully, most of your abilities."

She gave me a moment to digest what she'd told me. "What happened to you, Detective Myles, is that you had a blockage in one of the blood vessels that feeds blood, and therefore oxygen, to your brain. This is referred to as an ischemic stroke. Fortunately, you had a bit of luck on your side; your co-workers reported your speech and facial problems as soon as you arrived in emergency. Their description of your symptoms meant the ER doc was able to quickly conclude you most likely had a stroke. Thus, you were sent for a CT scan straight away. This allowed for quick detection of the blockage." Again, she paused to let me think about what she'd said. "The other lucky part of you being at work was that you got to the hospital very quickly. In fact, from what I heard, there was a police car practically lodged in the sliding doors of our emergency department!"

"These were both important factors, because in your case we were able to quickly identify the area in the brain where the blockage was and restore blood flow to the area. We used a specialized medication called recombinant tissue plasminogen activator—r-tPA for short. This is a common treatment and it's normally effective, but the key to its effectiveness is twofold: first, you need to get help quickly for it to be truly successful; a rule of thumb for us is within the first three to four hours. The second important thing is that you need to have the right kind of stroke for the treatment to work. In your case we were able to break up the blockage, so you were quite fortunate."

I didn't feel particularly lucky at the moment, but I let her continue.

"But you did have a period of time when oxygen was not getting to a couple of areas of your brain. Specifically, the blockage affected the left side of your brain in areas of the temporal and parietal lobes. That means your speech might be affected because one of the areas of the brain responsible for speech, called Wernicke's area, was without oxygen for a brief period of time. Also, because primarily the left side of your brain was affected, you will experience some difficulty operating the right side of your body. But over the next few days or even hours I expect that you will start to get progressively better." That was exciting to hear.

The doctor continued, "Progression of recovery depends on the individual. Everyone moves at their own rate. The nurse has already told me that you are having difficulty swallowing. This is called dysphagia. She also told me that you were having trouble drinking and speaking. These symptoms can be temporary and you may return to normal once your brain begins to heal. We often see some recovery after the stroke has subsided. This is what we call spontaneous recovery. Maintaining this recovery is our priority and ultimately your priority, of course. So, we will assist you medically, cognitively, and physically to not only maintain your gains but also to get you back to normal as soon as possible."

She paused again. "I should also tell you that the lack of oxygen to the brain causes neurons to die off. The extent of this damage will become more apparent in the next few days. The brain has a great ability to repair itself; I have seen this time and time again, and there are ways we can help you increase your recovery and get you back to one hundred percent. In fact, Detective, in your case, I'm hoping that with the active mind I know you have, and the recovery strategies we put in place will be highly effective. This hospital has adopted a new approach to treating stroke-related brain injuries and this unit is dedicated to treating patients like you. I understand that this is a lot of information to give you at this point, but I thought it best to tell you as much as I can up front so you're as informed as possible."

I nodded in agreement (I think). I *did* want as much information as possible and I had a number of questions that I could not ask at this point. Dr. White went on to explain that the specialized ward I was in offered a number of opportunities to engage in specialized treatment programs.

She also told me I would have a few MRIs and CT scans over the next week or so to determine how much damage there was and to ensure areas of damage were "reperfusing," which she said meant that blood was flowing properly again. She reassured me that they would do all they could and that I should get some rest for today. We would begin the treatment strategies as soon as possible.

As she was about to leave, she said, "I'm sure you will have a number of questions after I leave, and in due time, you can ask them." She also told me that a number of fellow officers had inquired about me, but she wanted to know if there were any family members who should be contacted. I shook my head no (again, I think) because I did not want my ex-wife or my daughter to worry about me. As for anyone else, I didn't want them to see me in such a state.

"Okay," Dr. White said, and gave me a pat on my leg. "Get some rest and I will see you tomorrow, and we will get you up and working." I gave her what I thought was a thankful look and she left.

For the next hour or so I went over in my mind everything Dr. White had said. She said I was lucky for couple of reasons related to the timing of my stroke treatment and the type of hospital I had been brought to. This made me wonder what would have happened if I had been alone or if I lived in a place where I couldn't get quick treatment. What if I was in a hospital that had limited knowledge of, or access to, the same types of treatments?

I gazed over at the woman on my right and began to wonder what her story was. How did she get here? I wondered about the bandage on her head. Did she have a stroke too? Since we were in the same ward, I figured she must have. I sarcastically congratulated myself. Good work, Detective.

CHAPTER 2
CASEY JOHNSON

Casey Johnson's life had consisted of a series of impulsive or ill-timed decisions. She had left home at seventeen when the opportunity arose. She felt the rules were unreasonable and there was so much to explore "out in the real world"; to be constrained by childhood rules was just too much to bear. And home life for Casey had not offered a supportive environment anyway. Her mother often yelled and ridiculed her as a way to make sure she got her household chores done. As for school, her mother believed its teachings held no value. She thought working was better experience and would give Casey more valuable life lessons. As for Casey's father, he was much older than her mother and Casey could not relate to him on any level; there was always an unbridgeable generation gap between them. This implicit distance meant that having actual distance between them would certainly not change their relationship, and it was another reason for Casey not to remain at home.

So Casey decided the best way to change her life was to change her location. She was young and naïve and assumed that changing where you were meant you could change your state of mind, change your luck, change your fortune, and run away from your problems. And for Casey, leaving home young did indeed help her keep a number of things from her childhood out of her mind.

This information I pieced together over the next day or so, as her sister came to engage in one-sided conversations with her, sometimes about very personal and deep topics and other times about the most mundane things, such as the lovely dress she had worn to their cousin's wedding ten years ago. The sister's intense monolog often included open-ended questions, such as why Casey had left all those years ago and how they had allowed themselves to spend so many years apart. It was mere guesswork at first, but over time I learned that she had indeed lived her life fast and hard.

***

Two days before her stroke, Casey woke up in her flat at her usual time: 3:00 PM. Today, however, was a special day for Casey; today was the day she had marked on her calendar that she was going to start her new exercise and diet program. So she started the day not as she usually did, which was with a chocolate chip muffin, a large cup of coffee (double cream, double sugar), and a handful gummy bears from a large jar she kept on her counter.

Instead, today she pulled from the fridge three large carrots, half a lemon, some red lettuce and kale, and half an apple. She threw it all in the blender with a little tomato juice and water, resulting in a drink unlike any she had ever tasted—and hoped not to taste again anytime soon.

Still, Casey was not faint of heart and she often stuck with things, for a while anyway. As Casey consumed her drink, she spread her last two rice cakes with a little almond butter packet she nabbed from a sample desk at the local supermarket. The almond butter was a godsend, she thought; otherwise, she was not sure she could have gotten her drink down and the taste out of her mouth.

After breakfast, Casey sat down on her brown leather couch. She had a one-room flat on the fourth floor of a converted factory. She stared out her floor-to-ceiling windows at the early-afternoon sun and the deep-blue sky. In this part of town, the view was mostly of industrial buildings, but on a clear day she could see the entire nearby park from her sleeping loft.

Today there was a lot of smog, and Casey could mainly see her reflection in the glass. She touched her worn face, feeling all her well-earned lines, and wondered how long it would be before she looked what she considered *old*. Years ago, she was used to passing for younger than her age, but that was many years ago now, and if anything, perhaps the opposite was now true.

Casey drank a lot on the weekends and smoked more while she drank. She used drugs recreationally, usually when her friends urged her along—she would try almost anything once. She liked to have fun, and she had no desire to be an exceptional or productive member of society. Casey's goal was mainly Casey; she liked it that way and tried hard to believe that all she cared about was herself. It was just easier that way.

Casey had been striking in her youth, with long black hair and deep brown eyes. She was a trim 5'8", with a small waist and large breasts, thanks to implants she had saved for years ago (and a little help from a boyfriend at the time). Casey liked to wear clothes that showed off what she had, and what she had paid for. Although she was never overweight, she was never the picture of health, and her usual exercise consisted of walking to work and back and taking the occasional flight of stairs. Casey's natural beauty and slim frame required little work to maintain, and thus long nights with liquor and cigarettes, topped off with fast food on her way home, were the norm. But she had come to believe her lifestyle was now starting to catch up with her, as she often felt out of sorts after those nights out.

WILLIAM J. TIPPETT

Casey plugged her iPod into her speaker system, deciding to go with a lighter mix. She often played such music on days after a rough night. Today's playlist included some Sugarland, Chantal Kreviazuk, and Portishead. After Casey put on the music, she sat down at her very stylish kitchen table to count her tips from the night before, as she did after every work night. But the count did not take long since it had been a slow night.

But she never lingered long on worrisome thoughts, like making ends meet, because she could not mentally afford to be that type of person, and it just wasn't fun to think that way. Casey was often guided by how much fun something might be. She was a hard worker, always had been, and currently she worked in a great bar. Being a bartender gave her a great non-taxable (in her view) cut of all the waitresses' tips, plus her own. Casey was not one to invest this "extra" money in anything secure (because that would not be fun). Instead, she preferred to spend it on things that made her happy. For instance, getting her hair done was a regular $350 trip to the salon. Adding a massage and a manicure at her favorite spa meant Casey's "maintenance" costs were high. Then there was her love for high-end everything—restaurants, shoes, pursues, the lot. After all that, and the rent on her fashionably decorated flat, there was not much left to save at the end of each month. But for Casey, if there was $100 in the bank she was ahead of the game.

After counting her tips, Casey would often curl up in her oversized chair with a cup of tea or coffee; today it was green tea. As Casey sat staring out the window listening to her morning music, she reflected on her to-do lists. Today, her thoughts took her, as they sometimes did, to the familiar territory of her regrets in life and the many mistakes she had made. She would never admit these out loud; mulling

22

them over in her head once in a while was an exercise in futility that Casey engaged in perhaps as a subconscious attempt to deal with unresolved emotional issues.

As Casey was dipping further into mental hopelessness as a result of this reflection, her phone rang. She gasped when she saw from the call display that it was her sister, Cassandra. Casey and Cassandra lived on opposite sides of the country, but that didn't hinder their ability to instantly engage in heated arguments. The distance only meant they couldn't actually see the eye-rolling they were both quite aware of.

Casey guessed what Cassandra was calling about before she even picked up the phone; undoubtedly, it was about Cassandra's husband, Bob. This was going to be the weekly "why Bob sucks" conversation—and it was. Casey braced herself to listen to the newest reason why Bob was a bad husband and how Cassandra had had it with him.

But before Cassandra could get into the details of why Bob should not be allowed to attend poker night again this month, the call was interrupted by a call from work. Although Casey hated taking calls from work, especially since she had just left there only a few hours ago, it was a welcome interruption. She said goodbye to Cassandra and switched to the incoming call.

The call was from the day manager, Diana, who said she needed Casey to come in earlier tonight. Rob, the daytime bartender, had to leave early and since he was part owner there was not much Casey could say except "I'll be there." Plus, she could use the extra money. Casey worked almost every night (except Sundays, when the bar was closed) from 8:00 PM. to 3:00 AM. She rarely got out of work much before four because of clean-up. Casey really didn't mind the work and she craved the nightlife, but the last few years had seemed to wear uncharacteristically on her. Most nights, she couldn't wait to get home and crawl into bed. When she was younger, Casey had crawled into many different beds. She would then grab a quick nap at home, shower, change, and go right back into work. She didn't have the strength for that anymore. Tonight, she had to start at six, which was going to make for a long night. Plus, tips at the dinner hour were crappy and hardly worth the extra time.

Casey often had to come in early for Rob, but today she was annoyed because she had planned to start at a new gym and had a meeting with a personal trainer this afternoon. Casey had been feeling a bit run down lately, and noticed she was sometimes a bit short of breath. This made her think that now was the time to get into better shape, but at forty-eight she wasn't sure it would be easy. She knew quitting smoking was a good start, but was not quite on board with that yet. Casey did not want to miss her appointment with her trainer, so she decided she would just go straight to work from the gym. Her meeting was at 4:45, which gave her only an hour and a quarter before she had to be at work; time was going to be tight, but she felt it was important to meet with the trainer even though she knew she would not have the time to complete everything that was needed today. She stuffed some work clothes into her gym bag.

Casey arrived at Complete Fitness five minutes late, but as she had signed up for the platinum package last week, she felt sure they would be forgiving. After changing into her workout clothes—black tights, a neon green sports bra underneath a loose-fitting black tank top—Casey was ready. She headed to reception to find her trainer. The tanned young blond with the six-pack abs behind the counter told Casey that her trainer, Luke, was waiting at the juice bar and pointed him out.

Casey went over and introduced herself. Luke was a well-built individual, though not tall by Casey's standards, and appeared to have virtually no body fat. He was wearing a tight-fitting long-sleeved gray tech shirt and black shorts with the Complete Fitness logo. Luke had sandy blond hair and looked to be about twenty-five. He gave Casey a hearty handshake and asked her to sit down. Luke began to explain to Casey, in very matter-of-fact terms, the program he had worked out for her.

"Casey, I have worked up a complete schedule for you for the next three months," he explained, "based on the goals and information you provided in your initial interview. I think, based on your age and current self-described level of activity, the best way to meet your goals will be for you to stick to a tight schedule of eating right and exercising four or five times a week, or possibly five or six depending on the duration and type of exercise you engage in each time." The expression on Casey's face changed slightly but Luke did not give her time to respond. "I've also made a list of foods we recommend and the calorie goal we should be aiming for each week, even though weight is not a particular issue for you. But based on what you've told us, I'm guessing you don't have a great level of fitness or otherwise you wouldn't be here."

Casey nodded slightly, which he took as acceptance and continued his bluntly honest introduction. "I also should highlight that we have had an increase in the number of older clients at the gym, and this is because the population is getting older and living longer, and a healthier lifestyle is really important to them, as it should be everyone. So I'm glad to see you're here early."

Casey felt that could have been a veiled attempt at a compliment, but it was difficult to tell from his expression. Luke then asked her, "Have you noticed a reduction in your cognition?" He then quickly rephrased the question as if she already had a cognition problem. "Do you find that you have a harder time thinking or working out problems?"

Casey thought it was a strange question for a personal trainer to ask, but answered anyway. "Well, I guess a little bit. But I'm sure none of us are as sharp as we were twenty years ago."

Luke explained that he had just completed his kinesiology degree and one of his focuses of study was the effects exercise can have on the brain and how exercise increases blood flow to the brain. He explained that the brain is a vascular organ and that developing a healthy body would also help develop a healthy mind. "So, a great side effect of getting into better shape can be sharper thinking. Exercise also has positive effects on high blood pressure and can reduce your chances of having a heart attack or stroke." Casey didn't make much of this information except to think, Great, maybe I'll be better at balancing my checkbook after I'm done this program.

After reviewing documents on the goals for a healthy lifestyle and a path to a better self, Luke completed the usual height, weight, and body-fat measurements. Casey's introduction to the program also included a tour of the weight machines, a demonstration of the proper techniques, and a test of her abilities. Meaning, Casey believed, that he felt it necessary to watch how pathetically few repetitions she could do on each activity.

Afterward, Casey was on her way to work with what seemed like a book's worth of material to review. Apparently, Luke liked his clients to also earn a degree as part of his program. Casey wondered if she and Luke might be headed for some rough water.

**

A day and a half later, Casey woke up feeling extra tired. She attributed it to staying out for after-hours drinks, topped off with a stop at the local diner for a nice, greasy breakfast, one of Casey's favorite activities after a night of drinking. She also had a significant headache, and reached for her bottle of aspirin. Casey noticed that oddly, the pain of the headache was radiating into her face as well. She'd never had a headache that did that. It was most uncomfortable, but she figured three or four aspirin and a big glass of water should help.

Casey went to the kitchen to get some water, and then opened her fridge to see what she had. She had made a grocery list based on some of the information she received from her personal trainer, but the only thing in the fridge was some leftover sushi from her takeout the other night and some of the ingredients she used to make her healthy shakes. She declined these and instead decided to grab a quick protein shake at Starbuck's before going grocery shopping.

Casey pulled on a pair of yoga pants and grabbed a sweatshirt and, just before heading out the door, picked up her large knapsack to carry her groceries, making her think she should add this to her weekly exercise plan. Casey was disappointed she had gone out for breakfast that morning, and vowed today things would change.

At the store, Casey spared no expense, buying organic whenever possible and grabbing items with a label claiming it was a "healthy option." Casey picked up as many of the items on her list as she could, but she discovered that many could not be found at a regular grocery store. In fact, when she asked a store clerk where she could find flaxseed, he replied that the sunflower seeds were in aisle six and moved off in a hurry to avoid other tough questions. Casey bought what she could; tomorrow she would head out to the health food store a few blocks from her place. But for today she was done with shopping and just wanted to go home and make something to eat, then hit the gym before work that night.

Casey got back at 4:45 PM and made herself an egg-white omelet, adding some fresh mushrooms, feta cheese, fennel, spinach, and garlic. She followed this with a homemade milkshake. Grabbing her gear, she headed to the gym, although she was not in the mood to start this new schedule—especially since her head was still hurting. In fact, this headache seemed to linger longer than usual. Often when she had a headache, she felt much better after eating, but not today. This one wanted to hang on.

At the gym, Casey did some light biking to start, but after twenty minutes she had had enough and decided to do some stretching in the mat room before getting changed and heading to work.

Casey got to work just a few minutes before her shift. It seemed no matter how early she left home she always got there right before her shift started. She thought miraculous forces of nature were involved to always make her arrive just barely on time, but she knew most of her co-workers just thought it was her lack of caring about time. She also knew some of them wished they could be as carefree as she appeared.

Casey got straight to work cleaning the bar area after the day shift, as she always did. Casey knew tonight was going to be a busy night. Casey may have appeared to be a carefree spirit, but when it came to her work she liked to have everything in her area organized and ready to go so that when it got busy, she could still be efficient. Casey had been doing this job a long time and she really knew her stuff—as bartenders go Casey was well known and never had a problem picking up a new position whenever she felt a need for a change. Proprietors liked her attention to detail and of course the increased revenue she generated on her shifts. Looking good and being good at your job went a long way in her field.

The nightly rush started as usual around eleven. Each night of the week had a different pattern. Casey knew that people went to work, she was sure of it, but sometimes it didn't seem that way—the bar could be filled and rocking on a Wednesday night, which never made sense to Casey, but she didn't care. The tips were good and it made the night go faster.

By around midnight the bar was nicely filled. Casey was on top of her staff and things were running smoothly, considering the organized chaos that occurs every night behind the bar. Casey had been taking two or three orders at a time, which was easy for her, but as she took the next order she didn't quite hear the customer. She asked him to repeat the order, but the words did not come out. Instead, it was a slur of syllables that made no sense. The customer asked loudly, "What?"

Casey did not comprehend what was going on, and she dropped the glass that was in her right hand. The crowd cheered when it smashed on the floor, as per usual bar etiquette. Casey didn't react; she was starting to feel numb. She could not feel her arm or hand. The customer was looking at her very strangely now because her face has become asymmetrical.

Two other bar staff were working with Casey, Josh and Rachael. Both hurried over because they knew something was not right with Casey. "Are you okay?" Josh asked, but Casey could not answer—no words would come out. She felt her legs lose their strength, and just before she fell, Josh grabbed ahold of her and sat her down at the back of the bar on a beer keg.

Josh called for the head waitress, Lynn. Josh was confused, because Casey was someone who was always in control. When Lynn came over, he said, "Something's very wrong with Casey. She won't answer, her face looks weird, and I had to help her down."

"Casey!" Lynn said sharply, right in Casey's face, but there was no response. Casey just stared. Lynn turned to Josh. "Did she take anything?"

"I don't know."

Lynn knew that Casey had experimented with drugs, but had never seen her under the influence at work—Casey was always on her game. "Help me get her to the office," Lynn said. Josh and Lynn essentially carried Casey to the office and laid her down on the couch.

Lynn didn't know what to do, didn't know if she should call an ambulance. If Casey was on something, would Casey get in trouble if Lynn called an ambulance? Maybe Casey would lose her job. She didn't want that, Casey was great to work with. Lynn decided she would just let Casey rest for a while, and maybe she would be okay.

After twenty minutes, Lynn came back to check on Casey and saw that nothing had changed: she still didn't respond to Lynn, and one side of her face looked like it had been pulled down. Lynn decided to call 911.

After first going to the wrong bar, the ambulance arrived twenty-six minutes later. All Lynn could tell the paramedics was that Casey had collapsed; she hadn't seen what had happened, and Josh was on break and Rachael was busy managing the busy bar by herself, so they couldn't help. Lynn did say that Casey had used drugs in the past, but she didn't know if she had taken anything tonight.

So all the paramedics could do was monitor Casey's pulse, blood pressure, and breathing as they loaded her up for the fifteen-minute ride to the hospital. As the medics were raising the gurney into the ambulance, Josh returned. "What's the matter with her?"

"We don't know. Did you see anything?"

"I was working at the bar with her when her face looked funny, kinda droopy on one side, and she dropped a glass. She seemed dazed and it was like she was having trouble speaking, just kind of moaning, really. I grabbed her and sat her down, and then we brought her to the office. And then she was pretty much out of it."

The paramedics looked at each other, right away realizing the situation was critical. As one rushed to the driver's seat, the other climbed in the back and said, "It's quite possible that she's had a stroke. Getting to the hospital now is most important. We'll take her to the Stroke Center at Lakefield." With that, the paramedic pulled the doors shut and the ambulance sped off, siren screaming.

Josh and Lynn were left standing on the sidewalk in bewilderment. "A stroke?" Lynn said. "Is that possible? She's only, like, forty-something. Aren't people that have strokes much older?"

Josh shook his head. "It must be something else."

Inside the ambulance, the medics radio in that they have a woman in her late forties who has most likely had a stroke and they are going to take her to the Stroke Center, which is fifteen minutes away at Lakefield General Hospital. "She's unconscious, breathing, but her blood pressure is low and breathing is shallow." Dispatch notified Lakefield of the incoming possible stroke, which triggered a new protocol: the on-call stroke neurologist was also notified of the incoming patient and would meet the patient in the ER.

Dr. Gerard Montoya's pager went off just as he was about to take a bite of his sandwich. He had been on call since 7:00 AM and after a full day of seeing patients and an evening full of paperwork he decided to go down to the café to grab a quick bite to eat. He liked how quiet it was at the hospital in the wee hours some nights. He could often find time to relax for a few minutes and catch his breath when he worked the on-call shift overnight.

But tonight was catch-up night, and he had a pile of charts to go through. Dr. Montoya was meticulous with his notes and he wanted his charts to always be up to date, so he worked hard to stay on top of them. He was a fellow at the hospital and was trying to make a good impression because there was an attending position coming up shortly and he was hoping to land it and thus be able to stay at the hospital.

He finished his sandwich quickly and called the hospital's locating desk. He was informed of the incoming patient with a suspected stroke; she was now experiencing seizures. Dr. Montoya had a bad feeling about this patient even before he hung up the phone. He knew from her age and the brief description of her symptoms that it was quite possible he was dealing with a hemorrhagic stroke. If that was the case, she may need surgery right away to stop the bleeding. He also knew that if there was a bleed and she had been delayed at all in getting to the hospital she could end up with significant impairments.

Dr. Montoya asked the switchboard to page a surgeon to meet him in the imaging department to help assess the level of damage. When Casey Johnson arrived to the ER, triage told the paramedics to take her right to the computed tomography (CT) suite. They signed her over, and nurses began prepping her for imaging.

Dr. Montoya was happy to see that Dr. Craig, the senior attending neurosurgeon, was on call tonight—he would be invaluable in helping decide the best course of action for this patient. Dr. Montoya was also a little intimidated by the older, more experienced doctor. Dr. Craig was an excellent surgeon, but like most surgeons he wanted to "get inside" a person and see things first hand rather than wait around for other interventions.

Fenton Craig entered the room briskly. He was in his early sixties, not a tall man, and wore heavy black-rimmed glasses. He greeted Dr. Montoya with a hearty handshake. "What do we have?" he said, leaving no doubt that his time was important and Dr. Montoya needed to explain, and now. Montoya quickly gave as much background on the patient as he had, and then reviewed the results of the Glasgow Coma Scale assessment that had just been done, as well as other standard data, while the CT images were coming up on the screen.

Dr. Montoya couldn't help feeling like he was back in med school, being tested, but Craig was thinking mainly about his upcoming vacation; his remaining focus was on the scans as they came up on the screen. As the images came through both physicians quickly saw the unfolding problem: the entire left hemisphere of the brain was filled with a dense black cloud: blood. It was not unusual for a bleed in the early stages to appear so large, but the size and extent of bleeding was still unknown. They knew something had to be done. But was it too late?

Craig knew he needed to get in there and drain the blood from the area to be able to save what he could at this point, and then work on locating the rupture to stop any more hemorrhaging if the vessel had not yet closed over. Craig turned to Dr. Montoya. "I need to get her into surgery right away and get a clip put on that. But I can't tell exactly where it is with all this blood pooling in the brain, so we need to open her up." Montoya knew there were other options but did not question Dr. Craig's request. He figured Dr. Craig was the patient's best bet at this point, so wished him luck and asked him to page him when the patient was in post-op. There was nothing more he could do right now.

CHAPTER 3
THOMAS BATTON

Thomas woke on Saturday, as he had many times before, with his wife, Ella, missing from their bed. She must have had trouble sleeping again. Thomas knew right where to find her. To avoid bothering Thomas, when Ella had a sleepless nights she went downstairs to the den to watch TV and then eventually fall asleep, spending half the night on the couch, snuggled up in the quilt she had made many years ago.

While she had been making the quilt, she said it was for Thomas, but he was fairly certain the only time he had used it was when he was sharing it with Ella. Thomas and Ella had been married for forty-one years and knew each other as well as two people could. They had raised three children in the three-bedroom home they had bought thirty-eight years ago, experiencing all the ups and downs a couple goes through in life, and they had always come through them together. They still lived in that quiet suburban home and enjoyed the simpler things in life: walks through the neighborhood, coffee at the local café, and dinner out with friends.

Thomas was a retired high school teacher who had spent almost thirty-three years teaching young minds the joys of math. He had been known as a captivating teacher with the ability to keep the kids' attention. He had a knack for finding a way to relate to every student individually and to show them why math was important.

Thomas's private passion was flying. He had learned to fly when he was a teenager, but had gone flying only occasionally when he was working. But that had changed since his retirement. When he retired, he had bought himself a gift, a used Cessna170, and since then he had spent many hours working on his plane. He loved getting up into the air whenever he could.

He also loved music and when he was not fiddling with various parts of his plane, from the upholstery to the engine (bits of which he often left around the house), he loved to listen to old records. He kept his collection of over a thousand albums in meticulous shape and perfectly organized, building special shelving for them that took up an entire wall in the basement, much to Ella's chagrin. Once in a while he was even inspired to try his hand at writing his own songs.

As a never-ending reader Thomas continued to enjoy learning new things. Once, just for fun, he had attempted to learn the 60,000 streets of London, like a taxi driver must to get his license there.[1] He had Ella test him on the best routes to get around London, as if she were traveling around town. He had read somewhere that London taxi drivers had bigger brains and an enlarged hippocampus so he thought this would be a great way to keep his brain active.[2] And hey—why not? So with his various hobbies, retirement was treating Thomas well.

Thomas stood 6'3" and had had wavy brown hair in his youth, but now his brown hair was in short supply next to the amount of gray on his head. He had been a good athlete and still loved to play many sports, so he was in good shape for sixty-nine and still mostly kept up with the younger guys on his hockey and baseball teams.

Ella, in contrast, liked to spend time with a good book these days. She liked their daily walks but was not much for organized sports anymore. Ella was just two years younger than Thomas and still a very striking woman if you asked any of her friends, but to compliment Ella on her looks resulted in her genuine protests. Ella was a slim woman with black hair, with a little help from the salon, which she liked to keep short. She had intense green eyes, which could be kind or piercing depending on her mood and intentions.

Thomas's morning started like any other. After waking Ella up, he went to the kitchen and put on the kettle for tea. Breakfast typically included fresh fruit, yogurt, and granola. On cold mornings they would sometimes have hot oatmeal with almond slices and honey. Breakfast was a good time to read the paper and catch up on the news before heading out for their morning walk. Their walks often included a stop at their favorite café for dark-bean espressos and lively conversation, hence the need to brush up on the preceding day's events. Thomas and Ella's route was about three miles, and they went out rain, shine, or snow.

Thomas helped Ella get her coat on, as he always did. Today Ella wanted to stop at the mall to have a look at a special on cotton fabric. She had in mind maybe making Thomas a new quilt for his birthday, a larger one that would be nice and cozy for him if he fell asleep on the couch. He maintained that this never happened but she knew it did, and quite often.

The pair headed out the door and started walking south to the biking and walking path that cut through part of their neighborhood. The path was in a treed area and it was difficult to see the houses from it, so it provided the illusion that they were in the woods. Except, of course, for the paved pathway, the lampposts, the benches, and the sounds of the city. Besides that, it was exactly like walking in the woods, Ella liked to believe.

They were about halfway through their walk when Thomas felt a sharp pain in his head. He grabbed his head and said, "Wow—that really hurts!" There was a bench nearby and he headed for it. He stumbled, almost dragging Ella to the ground.

"Thomas! What's the matter?" Thomas said nothing. Ella held his shoulders and said sharply, "What's wrong?"

Thomas was holding the right side of his head. He raised his left hand and held his finger up but it was a minute or two before he spoke. "Wow—that was like a really bad mini-migraine, one like I never felt before."

Ella was deeply concerned. "We better get you to the doctor today."

Thomas waved his hand dismissively. "No, no I'm fine now. I'm sure it was just a headache or something." He neglected to tell Ella that his vision was also blurred, nor did he explain the weakness he felt in his left arm. He had trouble speaking for a moment, but eventually he said, "I'm fine. It's eased off now. I'm sure I'm fine."

Ella looked skeptical but Thomas redirected the conversation, suggesting he might have a hot chocolate today and maybe cut back on his caffeine. "I'm sure it's just a little dehydration." Ella still looked worried as they walked on. Thomas secretly flexed his left hand, trying to get some feeling back.

When Thomas and Ella arrived at the café Thomas asked for water and a hot chocolate, forgoing his usual espresso. After placing his order he turned to Ella. "I likely haven't had enough water lately. I'm fine. I'll drink lots of water today." In solidarity, Ella ordered a flavored water.

They spotted some friends in the crowded café and joined them to discuss the day's top stories. The conversation progressed as usual, but Thomas couldn't quite engage. He was still thinking about what had happened to him. It made him think of his mortality and he wondered how Ella would cope when he was gone. Who would look after her? He wondered, too, if she knew how much he loved her. Thomas did his best to push these thoughts out of his mind for now and with effort returned to the conversation, which was now about property tax hikes and cuts to city services. Thomas concentrated on appearing engaged.

After an hour and a bit at the café, Thomas and Ella resumed their walk. Before they headed to the mall, Ella put her hand on Thomas's arm. "Do you want to go home and rest instead?" She sensed that something was not quite right with Thomas.

Thomas waved her off. "You know what Newton didn't quite say." She rolled her eyes. Yes, she knew. Thomas was fond of pointing out that Newton was often misquoted. "A body in motion tends to stay in motion." He started walking. "I don't want to rust up, Ella, so let's keep moving."

Despite Thomas's cavalier attitude, he himself was still quite concerned about what had happened; the pain had been extreme. He made a mental plan to call his doctor's office first thing Monday morning to schedule a checkup. He didn't say anything to Ella, though. He was going say he thought he would go see the doctor about the leg he hurt last week at hockey. Though Thomas suspected Ella would see through his ruse, she would nevertheless be happy he was going so the "reason" wouldn't matter.

Late that night, Ella rolled over and looked at the clock: 2:00 AM. She was wide awake. She debated whether she should get up or close her eyes and try to go back to sleep. Eventually, boredom won out and she went down to the den for some late-night TV.

Thomas was having the most wonderful dream. He was flying, but instead of being in his Cessna he was in an F-35 fighter. As a child, Thomas had always wanted to fly a fighter jet, but the closest he even came was a ride with a friend at the airfield who had an old Russian-made MiG-15. The freedom Thomas felt during this dream was unlike any he had felt in a long time.

Thomas woke at 6:25, a little earlier than usual. He lay in bed for a time and then finally decided he would get up and see if Ella had left the TV on again. He encouraged her to use the sleep timer but usually she forgot and the TV was often on when he went into the den in the morning. When Thomas approached the den, he could hear the TV. When he turned in to the room, he saw Ella snuggled on the couch in the fetal position, with "his" quilt tightly wrapped around her.

He liked finding her like this. She looked so peaceful and happy when she actually slept, as if she was making up for the times when she didn't sleep well. Thomas had read somewhere recently that if you can make up for lost sleep on weekends by sleeping in for an hour or two it helps reduce the chance of developing diabetes. But Thomas and Ella were retired so they could make up for it any day, and with that thought he sat down at her feet and turned on the morning news. He leaned over and gave Ella a big kiss on the check and a pat on the butt. Ella grudgingly opened her eyes. "Hi, honey," she said. "Did I not make it back to bed last night?"

Thomas laughed and said with mock surprise, "No, my dear, you did not."

After catching the highlights on the news Thomas headed to the kitchen to put on some tea and get breakfast ready. Ella sat up and was watching a health segment on how genes play a role in how one chooses a mate. The reporter was explaining that researchers had shown that one's genes predispose you to choosing a mate of similar height, and that's why the majority of couples are of a similar height. Ella shook her head. Maybe it's not genes, maybe it's the fact that people of similar height can better engage in meaningful eye contact and therefore better conversations. Just as Ella was thinking of ways to discredit this theory, she heard a crash in the kitchen. "Oh!" she said involuntarily. My teapot! What an oaf he can be sometimes.

She made her way to the kitchen, ready to give Thomas heck for breaking her teapot, but when she reached the doorway, she saw Thomas on the ground. Ella ran to him. She could see he was struggling to get up, trying to speak but only mumbling. She could see, too, that his face was drooping on the left side. He was struggling but his left arm was not moving at all. Ella let out a brief cry of panic. Her world was Thomas, and it was crumbling before her eyes. This is my rock, she thought, this is my man, nothing can happen to him.

Ella was holding Thomas, trying to understand him, trying to understand what was happening. She felt panic rising but pulled herself together. She looked at him, all of him, and remembered a lecture they had been to last year at the library, a presentation on stroke. It had reviewed the signs and symptoms. She remembered the slide showing how to identify a stroke—she remembered FAST.

"FAST," she said out loud, almost involuntarily, as the thoughts came together in her mind. FAST meant check for a drooping face, an arm that didn't work, poor stability, and trouble talking. "Thomas. I think I know what's happening." She looked in his eyes as he tried to understand. "You're having a stroke."

"I'm going to set you down. I need to call an ambulance right away." She eased him against the kitchen counter and kept talking to him as she went for the phone. "You remember that lecture we went to? You have all those symptoms. And remember? We need to get to the hospital immediately," she said as she dialed 911.

As soon as the dispatcher answered, Ella said, "My husband is having a stroke and I need an ambulance quickly." She gave their address as she sat on the floor beside Thomas. "Yes," she said into the phone. "He doesn't seem to be able to say anything. Yes, his left arm." She held his hand, waiting while the details were relayed to the paramedics that were already on the way. "Oh—right; of course." She turned to Thomas. "I have to go unlock the door." On her way back to Thomas, she grabbed the quilt from the couch, and when she reached him, she wrapped it around him.

Ella stayed on the line with the dispatcher until the paramedics arrived, all the while comforting Thomas. The paramedics arrived within minutes, but those minutes stretched unbearably. She was holding her whole world in her arms. How fragile life is, she thought as the medics were placing Thomas on the gurney, as Ella was describing what had transpired. As one paramedic started a main IV line and attached a blood pressure cuff and pulse monitor, the other spoke to Ella. "Ma'am," she said, "we believe your husband is having a stroke and we need to get moving to the hospital right away." Ella nodded. The paramedic continued. "Please grab your coat, keys, whatever you need—we're leaving immediately."

Ella pulled a coat over her nightgown, stuffed her feet into her sneakers, and grabbed her purse. She locked the front door and the medics lifted Thomas into the ambulance. She climbed in after them. The paramedic in the back with her was so young that Ella thought she must just be out of school, but she was pleased the young medic was talking to Thomas, explaining what they were doing and what was happening. The paramedic moved efficiently, updating her partner who was driving, who in turn was updating the hospital.

The young paramedic told Ella, "We're en route to Lakefield General, which has a designated Stroke Center and is the best place we can go at this point." Her tone was reassuring. "The trip isn't long; we should be there in a few minutes. Our goal right now is to keep your husband comfortable and monitor him for any complications on the way. When we get there he's going straight into secondary triage."

That was a relief to Ella, since she had waited many hours in emergency rooms with her girls for various things over the years. The paramedic looked at Ella and continued. "We're going to move fast when we get there and I'm going to ask that you exit through the side door." She pointed to her right. "Wait till we get your husband out the back and then just follow us in." Ella nodded, and squeezed Thomas's hand.

The ambulance reached the hospital within minutes, to Ella's relief, considering the heavy Monday morning traffic. As soon as they reached the emergency entrance, the driver jumped out and before Ella could get to her feet the back doors were open. Ella rose quickly and went through the side door as instructed. Thomas was wheeled straight through the emergency waiting room into the emergency triage area. Ella listened closely as the paramedics relayed the information to a doctor who appeared to Ella to be no more than sixteen; Ella assumed the young doctor to be a resident.

The resident nodded as the paramedics explained the situation. A registration clerk approached Ella. "Can we get some information to admit... are you the patient's...?"

"Wife, yes," said Ella. She answered the clerk's questions, keeping her eyes on Thomas. The paramedics transferred Thomas to the hospital bed. The young paramedic handed the quilt to Ella and gave her a reassuring look as the medics left. "Thank you..." Ella gave a small wave and they were gone. Wow, thought Ella, and on to the next one.

The resident physician asked the clerk which stroke neurologist was on call.

"Dr. Pattern just came on."

"Please page him at once." With that he disappeared to another part of the hospital without saying a word to Ella or Thomas.

About ten minutes later a new physician arrived. He went directly to Thomas and appeared to check his vital signs. "I'm Dr. Pattern—Eli," he explained as he began to look Thomas over. "I'm a clinical neurologist. I'm going to do my best to look after you. In a couple minutes we're going to transfer you to our Stroke Center, and we're going to get a CT scan done on you so we can get an idea of what we're dealing with, okay?" He looked at Ella, who nodded. The doctor continued to explain the process. "When did his symptoms start?"

"Right around 7:00 AM," Ella told him.

Dr. Pattern looked at his watch. "Okay, great. He got here quickly and that's a good start." A nurse poked her head into the doorway and nodded at the doctor, and two orderlies entered. "We're going to take him up now," the doctor said to Ella. "If you want to complete your registration, I'll come back to the secondary waiting room and update you when I know more." And with that, Thomas and Dr. Pattern were gone.

Ella didn't feel she was in any state to deal with hospital bureaucracy, but she reluctantly went to the desk and talked to the registration clerk, providing all the information the hospital required to ensure it got paid, which sometimes appeared to be the priority.

Ella returned to the secondary waiting area, where she alternately sat and paced for about forty minutes. Finally, Dr. Pattern re-appeared. He sat down, motioning for Ella to do the same, and got right to the point. "What we saw on the scan was a blockage in one of the brain's arteries. That's what we call an ischemic stroke, which is much better than the other kind, a hemorrhagic stroke."

"Will he be okay?"

"We are keeping a close watch on him and we've started him on some medication that we hope will resolve his blockage. I'm actually hoping for some improvement shortly."

Ella slumped with relief.

"But," Dr. Pattern continued, "to be sure he's improving we'll do a CT angiogram very soon so we can get a better look at what's going on with the blockage and see if it's being resolved." The doctor paused for a moment to let Ella absorb the information, then continued. "Also, Mrs.

Batton, I want you to know that our senior attending physician, Dr. White, is in already and she'll be assisting me with your husband's care. She's the best we have in the city so he's in good hands. She'll be coming down to see Mr. Batton shortly and I'll brief her on the situation."

"Okay, but..."

"When we know more, I'll come right out and let you know." He stood and turned to go.

Ella stood as well. "Before you go... thank you. For all your help. Can I... can I be with Thomas? I'm sure he wants me there."

Dr. Pattern said, "Normally, I would say yes. We like loved ones to be around the patient. But we are keeping him in an area where we can perform imaging during the treatment process, so family can't go in there. You can watch through the window, but it's not the best vantage point." He could see her disappointment. "I think right now, let's get this figured out, and we'll come right back and get you as soon as possible."

Ella was not happy with his response but she did not want to cause any trouble or confusion with Thomas's care. So she sat. And she waited. She got up and paced a lap of the room and sat back down. She leaned back, closed her eyes, and rested her head on the wall. She thought over what the doctor had said. He had seemed hopeful. She tried to think about that. Then she sat upright with a jolt. The kids! She rummaged in her purse for her phone but realized she had left it on the kitchen counter. But there was a payphone in the waiting lounge. Ella gave a half smile. It was as if the hospital knew people in this room would not be at their most organized. She stuffed coins into the phone and called Susan, the oldest of their three daughters.

"Susie, it's your mother. Um, I'm at the hospital—it's Dad. He's had a stroke... Yes, thank God... No, he was awake... Well, I don't know; they won't let me go in right now, they're doing scans or something. They're going to come and tell me later. But this one doctor said it was not the bad kind of stroke, so maybe. Listen, can you call Lindy and Carrie and let them know?... But you're at work, I don't want... Okay. Yes, sixth floor I think. Thanks, Susie."

Susan had told Ella that she would come to the hospital. Despite her protest, Ella was relieved that Susan was on the way. That feeling of relief enabled her to leave the lounge and go downstairs to get a cup of coffee. The walk did her good, but she quickly returned to the waiting area, not wanting to miss the doctor.

About half an hour after Ella returned to the waiting area, a middle-aged doctor approached, her long white coat floating behind her as she moved with great speed. Ella wondered if this was Dr. White. She hoped so; the woman exuded confidence.

"Mrs. Batton?" Ella nodded. "I am Evelyn White. I just wanted to come and update you on your husband's prognosis."

"Please call me Ella." They shook hands.

"Ella." They sat down, and Dr. White began a rapid report. "So your husband has indeed had a stroke, as I assume Dr. Pattern told you. When he was brought to the hospital we did a quick assessment, the National Institutes of Health Stroke Scale, and his score was eighteen. That's not in the severe range, which is about twenty-nine and above,[3,4] though he was still in a range we would deem as moderate risk. Our first course of action was to proceed with tPA therapy, which Dr. Pattern did." The doctor noticed Ella's blank look. "tPA is a medication we use to help with a blockage in a blood vessel. Your husband has had what we call an ischemic stroke, which means he has a blockage in an important artery that feeds the brain."

Ella nodded slowly. "Okay..."

"tPA is tissue plasminogen activator. It's a thrombolytic drug that's helpful in breaking up clots or blockages such as what your husband was experiencing. Dr. Pattern thought, and rightly so, that because you reached the hospital quickly, in less than our typical three-hour window for using this medication, that this treatment would be most effective, and he hoped we would see some changes very shortly after we gave it to Mr. Batton. However..."

Ella's shoulders sank. There's always a "however."

"We did not see the desired response, so I ordered an angiogram. That showed a blockage in the right carotid terminus."

Ella gave a slow shake of her head to indicate she had no idea what this meant.

Dr. White explained. "That's a section of the carotid artery that runs through the neck," she pointed to her neck as she explained, and drew her finger up to the side of her head. "It feeds the brain's main arteries. Near the top of this artery is the area I'm speaking of, and a section that it feeds is the middle cerebral artery, which is a major artery supplying blood to the brain. In Mr. Batton's case this happened on the right side of his brain, so that's why you saw symptoms on his left side."

She gave Ella a moment to process. "I was able to insert a microcatheter into Mr. Batton's artery, which we call intra-arterial thrombolysis—IAT—and I was able to administer rapid localized treatment of a thrombotic medication directly to the area being affected, and a low dose of this medication directly to the affected area is ideal. This treatment takes a bit of time, so I'm sorry I couldn't come out to speak to you sooner."

"It's quite alright—I would rather Thomas be well looked after than you wasting time explaining to me every step you were taking." But her strained voice revealed that Ella was still tied up in knots inside, since Dr. White had really not told her how Thomas was actually doing. But she quickly added, "Please go on."

Dr. White finally realized that Ella was on pins and needles. "Oh my—I'm so sorry. I haven't even told you how he's doing. Your husband is doing quite well now."

Ella sighed with relief.

Dr. White continued her explanation. "After we'd treated the area directly, after about an hour we started to see recanalization of the area, which means that the blood began to flow again and the MCA, the middle cerebral artery, was receiving a good flow of blood and so his brain was being fed again. We will know more in a while, but this is great news and everything is working again, as it should."

"Thank you, Dr. White. Thank you so much." Ella paused before she asked, "What does this mean for him in the future? I know people that have had strokes, and some seem really... impaired, and have problems doing basic things. What do you think I can expect with Thomas?" She paused. "Will he... will he be okay?"

"I understand your concerns. But I can't give you any guarantees about his functional recovery, especially at this stage. And everyone's brain is a little different, so it's difficult to compare recovery rates or understand how one person will recovery versus another.

"But what I can do is tell you about the research in cases like Mr. Batton's, specifically with patients that arrive at the hospital quickly, like Mr. Batton did. He was treated almost immediately, and in combination with his current level of health, which I saw from his history is quite good, that makes a huge difference in recovery for almost any illness. So well done to both of you for staying healthy and active. Sometimes my work looks miraculous but it's the person themselves that makes the greatest difference in a lot of cases.

"Anyway, the research suggests a very good prognosis for recovery because of these factors. Some research in this area indicates that returning to normal function is not out of the question and with a little work a good goal to aim for."

"A normal recovery? Really? Dr. White, are you telling me it's possible that Thomas could be back to his old self without... issues?"

"Yes, it is, Mrs. Batton—Ella. It is possible. But I was explaining the general upside; there are also downsides to recovery, and Mr. Batton may have some deficits. We really don't know yet."

Ella stopped her short, holding up her hand. "No need to think of the negative. I will focus on the positive outcome we can achieve, and I'll let Thomas know that it's up to him to help me get him back on track."

Dr. White could see Ella's resolve and she was quite encouraged. Many times family members, especially spouses, fall apart and can't see the big picture.

"Ella, one more thing. I should also let you know that here at Lakefield General, as a dedicated Stroke Care Center, we have established ties with researchers from the university and have a number of ongoing rehabilitation programs available to patients such as Mr. Batton. I'll get you a list of our current projects." She paused and looked around the room, as if only now becoming aware of their surroundings. "Are you alone? Is there anyone you can call?"

"My daughter—one of our daughters is on her way." Ella gratefully shook Dr. White's hand and gave her a quick hug.

Before Dr. White left she said, "Mr. Batton is resting quietly now. We've placed him in one of our four-bed stroke wards. Very soon the stroke nurse will come and collect you and show you where he is. I will come see both of you in a while. Should you have any questions in the meantime, Dr. Pattern is still on the unit and is looking after the patients on the ward today."

Ella did have a question, she realized. She was wondering about the strange headache Thomas had had the day before. Just as Dr. White was going through the door, Ella took a step forward. "Doctor? Do you have a moment? I don't know if this might be important."

Dr. White turned back to Ella. "Yes?"

Ella hesitated. "I was wondering... Yesterday, Thomas had a—I don't know; a strange headache."

"Okay," Dr. White said, encouraging Ella to go on.

"It was very sudden, and seemed unusually painful. And he stumbled, when he went to sit down. Just for a moment he seemed... just not right. But it went away, and we continued our walk. Might that have been something to do with what happened today?" And then she added in a weak voice, "Should we have gone to the hospital?"

Ella noticed the doctor glance quickly at her watch, and felt bad for delaying her. But Dr. White sat down, and so did Ella.

"Of course I can't say because I wasn't there to examine him, but given what happened today, it might—*might*—have been a transient ischemic attack, or TIA; they're often called mini-strokes. It's called a mini-stroke because the symptoms are similar to what you would have in an actual stroke, but much shorter, like sometimes less than five minutes.[5,6] So that sounds like what happened to Thomas yesterday, but again, I can't know for sure. The other thing with a TIA is that you often recover with no ill effects, so you have all the functionality and faculties you had before the event."[5,6]

"Yes, he was fine for the rest of the day."

Dr. White nodded. "Because the person regains all their ability after just a short interruption, but the event itself can be quite scary for a while, people tend to want to just carry on as if nothing happened. But TIAs are a red flag, letting us know that something is not right. It is a very distinct warning sign that a stroke could be around the corner.

"So yes, we would say that you should get checked out right away if something like that happens. Someone who's had a TIA has a significantly increased risk of having a full-on stroke in the near future—as much as ten times the risk, in fact."[7]

"Oh my—that much?"

"A medical exam is also important because it's possible that the reason for the TIA is an underlying condition that's treatable—arterial fibrillation, for example."

"I've heard of that."

"It's a condition where your heart beats irregularly; we also call it arrhythmia. It's often related to heart disease and vascular disease. And that's just one condition that can affect the cardiovascular system and so creates risk of a stroke. There are other conditions that can increase your chance of having a stroke. So people need to get anything weird checked out."

"Thank you. I guess, then, that we should have come in. And maybe we..." Ella felt she might break down. "Maybe we could have prevented this?"

"There's no way to know. Because it happened just yesterday, even if we had started medication that day, or done some other intervention, it might not have made any difference—it might not have had enough time to take effect. We might not have even had a diagnosis by this morning." She put her hands-on Ella's shoulders. "This is not your fault. What happened yesterday happened yesterday. Focus on now. He's doing well."

Ella nodded weakly as the doctor rushed from the room.

CHAPTER 4
BRUCE GRAFTON

The day started like most other days for Bruce Grafton. He woke up in the bunk of his Kenworth truck, sat up, stretched out his arms, and yawned. He looked out the mud-spattered passenger window to his right at the beautiful lake he had parked beside last night. Normally his view when he woke up was of the side of another truck at some dusty truck stop, or sometimes just a brick wall. Other times, an endless highway.

But last night he had been fortunate enough to find an excellent pull out with a small park on the edge of a large lake. There were a few spaces for trucks to stop here, and Bruce found one of the best spots he had had in a while. He slept well, as he usually did, with the hum of his diesel engine keeping his battery charged and his bunk at the perfect temperature. Bruce pulled on his pants and coat and jumped down out of his truck with his shower bag in hand and crossed the park to the restrooms a short distance away. Wow, Bruce thought. If I could only find a rest stop like this every night.

Bruce used the washroom, but the shower wasn't very hot. Oh well; he knew everything couldn't be perfect. In a way it was a comfort, because if the shower was his biggest problem, he would have a good day. Bruce shaved and put on a new set of clothes. As he looked in the mirror at his wrinkled face, he smiled and thought, what a great start to the day. He went back to his truck, threw his bag in, and decided that before taking off for the day, which he had to do very soon, he would take a quick walk along the water.

As he walked he thought how great it would be to just hang out by the lake instead of facing another day driving fifteen or sixteen hours, depending on how he could work his official log book. He felt how sore his back was. Over the past ten years or so his metabolism had really slowed and spending so much time just sitting had led to a significant weight increase—he had put on, he figured, around twenty-five or thirty pounds. That was hard on his back. His stomach had grown a fair amount. He put his hands on it now, which made him think about how when he was young, he had been such a thin guy, and he could eat whatever he wanted and hardly put on any weight. Things had certainly changed.

Bruce had always been a trucker, just like his dad. When you leave school after grade eight, there are not too many choices out there. The money had always been good, though, especially for hard workers, and Bruce certainly was a hard worker. He had put in more miles than any other driver in the company over the past ten years, an accomplishment he was proud of, but a record like that comes at a cost. The cost for Bruce was his family and, looking down at his stomach, he realized maybe it was also his health. Long trips, limited time to eat, a lack of healthy food, and limited time to exercise on the road, he knew, would take their toll on his health. Whatever. Healthy people got sick too, he knew that much. And with that last thought Bruce looked at his watch and headed for his truck.

Bruce had a pickup this morning at a cookie factory and he wanted to be early so he didn't have to wait to get loaded and he could get out on the road before the other trucks got there. He knew there was a truck stop just a few minutes away so he could grab his breakfast to go and eat while his truck was being loaded.

The special of the day at the truck stop was two eggs with bacon, ham, cheese, and tomato on a toasted Kaiser bun, with a large hash brown potato on the side—he loved those things—and a large coffee. Bruce ordered his usual coffee, triple sugar, triple cream. He thanked the waitress, gave her a wink and a good tip when she handed him the bag, grabbed a few salt packets for his hash brown, and headed out.

Bruce was happy to get to the factory in plenty of time but as he pulled to the back of the building he realized he was second in line for loading. It looked like the first trucker had slept here last night. Bruce was annoyed that he had to wait for the other truck to be loaded ahead of his, but it wouldn't cost him that much time. He ate his breakfast while he waited and got his paperwork filled out.

Shortly after Bruce finished up his paperwork, he was able to back in and get loaded. He watched as they loaded the skids, making sure they were careful. After all, though Bruce worked for a trucking company it was not a company truck, it was his. As an owner-operator his truck and trailer were his livelihood.

Bruce chatted with the loading dock supervisor as the skids filled the truck. Bruce was a charismatic, outgoing guy and always seemed to find a way to discover what people were passionate about and talk about it with them. After Bruce was loaded the dock supervisor threw

Bruce a few slightly squashed bags of cookies. "Damaged! Have a good trip." Bruce often got boxes of this and that—perks of the trade. I'll take it! he thought.

Bruce climbed into the cab and began his 520-mile trip, which would include two stops. As Bruce got onto the interstate, he looked at the cookies he had been given and was thinking about the conversation he had two weeks ago with his physician, Dr. Kerran. Bruce had been to see the doctor because in the months before this visit, Bruce had noticed he was feeling more fatigued than usual and was having trouble just sitting and driving. He also noticed that when he was helping out unloading the truck or making repairs, he was having trouble catching his breath.

In addition, one night a few weeks earlier, when Bruce had splurged and got himself a nice hotel room, he had decided to use the hotel gym. After about fifteen minutes on the elliptical, he felt like his heart was going to beat out of his chest. He stopped. If this was what exercising was like, to hell with it. It wasn't worth it.

Though Bruce was a "man's man" and as tough as they came, he was aware that something was not right and though men of his generation generally didn't go to the doctor unless they were bleeding from the head, Bruce thought better of it this time and decided to go see Dr. Kerran.

Dr. Kerran took the opportunity to complete a number of tests on Bruce, including an echocardiogram. He was obviously concerned about Bruce's heart, based on what Bruce had told him. So Bruce had also mentioned that one night a couple of months ago he had significant chest pain and he lay in his bunk unable to move for hours. "But," Bruce explained, "it was okay. It eventually passed and I was fine in the morning."

Dr. Kerran had shaken his head. "Bruce, you most likely experienced a mild heart attack. You should have come to see me, or anyone, right away."

Bruce had replied, "I took a few aspirins and as I said I was fine by morning. There was no point in wasting anyone's time, especially mine, Doc."

Dr. Kerran had told Bruce that his echocardiogram showed a significant increase in muscle tissue in Bruce's left ventricle. He explained that this was scar tissue on his heart, suggesting that Bruce had indeed had some sort of "cardiac event," as the doctor had suspected.

"So what does that mean?" Bruce had asked.

"You most likely have developed a condition called left ventricular hypertrophy, which is caused by a few things, including your medical history. First, Bruce, your weight gain over the years is a significant concern, as I've mentioned on more than one occasion—it will have contributed to this condition. Second, you smoked for many years, and obviously smoking is an underlying cause of many significant health problems. It's directly linked to cardiovascular disease, resulting in a two- to fourfold increase in your chance of experiencing a cardiovascular event. In addition, 80% of smokers will develop illnesses such as COPD..."[8]

"Which is...?"

"Chronic obstructive pulmonary disease. It's eventually fatal. The rate of developing certain cancers is even higher."

Bruce had thought about those higher-than-80% rates. He had been dumbfounded that just having a few cigarettes a day could do that to your health, even after quitting.

Dr. Kerran had continued his lecture. "Third, you have high blood pressure, which can certainly contribute to this condition." Bruce had had high blood pressure pretty much his entire life but had never bothered to try to get it under control. Sitting in Dr. Kerran's office, he had started to put it all together and wonder what it meant. Was he going to die? What should he do? But it was probably too late anyway.

Dr. Kerran had gone on to explain that Bruce needed to change the way he ate. He was going to have to eat much better, and he would have to try to stick to a low-sodium diet. He had to get more exercise. "Just increasing your daily walking as little as forty-five minutes will help a fair bit," Dr. Kerran had said, "but you need to make an effort, Bruce." The doctor had prescribed some medication for Bruce's blood pressure. He had stressed that Bruce needed to make changes and now was the time to make them—or he may not be around much longer.

That conversation with Dr. Kerran had stayed with Bruce quite vividly. Bruce remembered that the doctor had explained that being obese was a factor related not just to heart problems but to stroke, and this concerned Bruce because his mother had died of a stroke. And she had been heavy. Dr. Kerran had also told Bruce recent research had shown that sitting for long periods was really bad for one's health, similar to the effects of gaining a lot of weight. Sitting was now bad for you! Bruce had to laugh at this because his job involved sitting literally for hours on end. That, combined with the fact that quick accessible foods were generally fast foods, made weight gain seem inevitable to Bruce. There was nothing he could do about it.

Dr. Kerran had pushed back. "You need to stop every few hours and walk around, do some stretching. And when you've stopped for the night, you need to get some exercise—just walking is a good start."

Bruce had nodded. But he couldn't believe the number of problems ganging up on him. He could never deal with them all. He wondered why he should even bother. What was the point? If he got on top of one, another would get him anyway. Dr. Kerran had handed him his prescriptions. "Come back and see me in three months and we'll see how you're doing."

***

Tony Kerran sighed as Bruce Grafton left his office. He saw a lot of patients like Bruce, which was one of the reasons he had recently entered his practice in a large study that involved stroke research. The study had focused Dr. Kerran's attention on cases like Bruce's and enabled him to provide patients with the information he had given Bruce to help them make lifestyle changes.

Dr. Kerran had been reviewing a number of journal articles related to stroke and stroke prevention. Some of the topics covered were the risk factors, such as being overweight, and associations between cardiovascular disease and other topics, like levels of sodium intake for a given population. Dr. Kerran realized that although the public generally accepted the fact that many of these factors contributed to strokes, people also believed that the effect each factor could have on a population was minimal. But nothing could be further from the truth. International reviews on the intake of sodium suggested that daily sodium intake should be under five grams, and perhaps a range of two to three grams a day would be acceptable.[9] But on average around the world, most populations easily exceed six grams per day, far above daily requirements. The research suggested that a significant reduction in salt intake for a whole population could mean a large reduction in cardiovascular disease. It had even been suggested that a reduction in salt intake to below six grams per day could mean a decrease in blood pressure of several points, especially in people who already have high blood pressure.[10]

One study of salt consumption around the world showed that in Asian nations, higher levels of sodium intake are a result of the style of cooking used historically, including the use of soy sauce and other high-sodium products. In Western Europe and North America the largest contributor to sodium intake for the general population is items such as baked goods, cereals,[9] and prepackaged foods designed to be preserved for great lengths of time. And people don't often think of baked goods—cookies, say—as high sources of sodium.

Dr. Kerran had always dealt with weight concerns in his clinic, but as the years had progressed, he had begun to see more and more patients who were struggling with weight gain. He'd seen patients try all manner of approaches to losing weight. One thing he knew was that skipping meals did not help weight loss and in fact only contributed to the storage of fat. He had seen with countless patients that cutting down on food could help them lose weight, but it made them hungry all the time so it never lasted; they would go back to eating the same foods, in the same amounts, if not more.

With these growing concerns, a lot of people were experiencing cardiovascular events (obstructions in the heart and blood vessels): heart attacks, strokes, mini-strokes, coronary artery disease, and aneurysms. Though recent research had shown that death rates related to cardiovascular disease had declined, they were still quite high. For example, in the United States there was, on average, one death every thirty-nine seconds as a result of it. In the US, one of every eighteen deaths was stroke related.[11]

Factors often contributing to death from stroke included characteristics such as those Bruce Grafton had: smoking, being overweight, sitting for long periods, and lack of exercise. But Dr. Kerran was hopeful. Modern medicine had been able to mitigate the effects of stroke-related events to a certain extent, reducing death rates (though not the number of "events"). Advances in medicine could assist in managing these patients and even reduce the negative consequences of a stroke. Although strokes persist, their management in recent years had been much more effective.

The doctor also knew, however, that this greater management of stroke-related events came at a cost. The costs directly and indirectly associated with stroke, both for healthcare and society (such as labor and care costs), was believed to be about $286 billion in the US alone in 2007.[11] This made Dr. Kerran think of Bruce and the impact a stroke might have on him. Since he had little family support, if he experienced a significant stroke, it would create a large impact—on him, on his livelihood, and on the economy.

***

Bruce had been running his last conversation with Dr. Kerran over in his head for the past two weeks, and the cookies in the crumpled bags sitting on the passenger seat beside him brought the conversation to the forefront of his mind again. He wondered if he should just give the cookies away at the next truck stop. He sighed. What was the point? That wouldn't change anything.

As Bruce drove, he took a few sips of coffee, which tasted great today. He thought the coffee would go great with something sweet. And so, he opened the first bag of cookies. He resolved that he would just have one or two. But before Bruce knew it they were gone, the whole bag was gone. Feelings of guilt and failure followed, as they often did. His lack of self-control upset Bruce very much. He lowered the passenger window and threw the remaining bag of cookies out of it. Now he felt guilty about littering.

Bruce's feelings were, of course, not uncommon for people trying to lose weight. Thinking that just one or two cookies won't hurt, and then realizing the whole bag was gone, starts the cycle of guilt, failure, and depression, leaving people believing they don't have the willpower to fight their urges and they should just accept that they are going to be overweight forever. Bruce had experienced these feelings many times. Even when he had tried to diet and managed to lose a few pounds, like so many others he then thought it was okay to treat himself. But that again resulted in overindulgence and he ended up right back where he started, or worse.

Bruce believed that severe dieting was the only answer but it never worked. Dr. Kerran had told him that dieting was not the answer and that only permanent lifestyle change could maintain weight loss. But Bruce felt he was too old to make those big changes and he didn't think he should have to deny himself all the things he liked to eat. What was going to be was going to be.

Bruce dropped off his delivery at about 9:00 PM in an industrial area just outside the town of Lakefield. He felt he was lucky for two reasons: first, he was the last truck allowed into the dock so he got his deliveries off ahead of schedule, and second, his delivery was right across from a buffet restaurant. After eating only a bag of cookies since breakfast, Bruce was seriously hungry. He'd decided not to eat anything else for lunch as "punishment" for eating the cookies.

Bruce believed in punishment and reward: just as he deprived himself of lunch because of the cookies, he also believed that if he went for a thirty-minute walk he was entitled to a treat, which was often a big bowl of ice cream or something else so calorie-laden that his walk didn't come close to burning half of the calories. He remembered his walk that morning and parked in the mall where the restaurant was located.

It was a great spot because he would be able to park there all night and after dinner he could go right to bed. The irony of the buffet being right beside a large gym was lost on Bruce. He also didn't notice the healthy-eating chain restaurant a little farther down the plaza. Bruce couldn't wait to get to that buffet. After he ordered his drink, he bypassed the salad bar and headed straight for the hot food because he was hungry for "real food."

Bruce was so full after dinner he went right back to his bunk to lie down and rest. He couldn't wait to get his belt undone, straining as it was on its last notch.

***

Bruce's alarm clock went off at 5:30 AM. He woke still feeling a little bloated from last night's meal, but realized that if he was going to drive all day he should pick up some breakfast anyway, especially coffee. He yanked on some track pants and a sweatshirt and jumped down out of his truck. He made his way to the coffee shop in the plaza.

As he got back into his truck with a jumbo double-cream coffee and a bag containing an egg-and-sausage sandwich, a couple of hash browns, and a chocolate cruller, Bruce thought about how his doctor had told him he needed to eat healthier. He knew that meant avoiding fried foods and high-calorie desserts but those were the things he liked to eat. He didn't want to eat salad.

As he sipped his coffee, he thought, you know, it just doesn't matter. Something's gonna get me eventually. Something's gonna get us all. Why not enjoy our time here, and eat what we want? As he sat in his cab, he felt his breathing become a bit labored. He suddenly felt incredibly tired, but there was no time to rest. He needed to get on the road. It was almost 6:00 AM.

Bruce checked his GPS for the nearest truck stop on his route so he could hopefully grab a shower. As he began to pull out of his parking space, he felt dizzy, *very* dizzy, and something seemed wrong with his vision. He knew he couldn't drive till this passed. He immediately stopped and reached for the bright-yellow air-brake button to ensure all wheels were locked up. Jumbled thoughts ran through his mind: what was happening, did anyone know where he was, how would he get help, where was his phone? He fumbled briefly, looking for it. Why was this happening, what...? Just after he had set his brakes, Bruce passed out on his steering wheel.

Bruce lay slumped in his cab for over an hour before another trucker pulled into the parking lot, planning to get breakfast at the coffee shop. The driver pulled up beside Bruce's rig and when he looked over, he saw Bruce. Drivers sometimes caught a nap in their seats while waiting around but it was not normal to see one draped over the wheel like that.

The driver got out and knocked on Bruce's door. Bruce did not move. The other driver knocked again, loudly. "Hey there!" Still no response. He tried the door, which opened. He stepped up and gave Bruce a hard shove, which didn't rouse him—the guy flopped like a doll. The driver knew it was bad but didn't want to get mixed up in it; maybe this passed-out guy was on drugs or something. He knew that if he stayed around, he would be answering questions for who knew how long and he'd end up behind schedule. So he used the payphone in the coffee shop to place an anonymous call to emergency services. He moved his truck to the parking lot exit and waited. Within a few minutes he saw an ambulance arrive, and went on his way.

The ambulance attendants found Bruce non-responsive but alive. They located his pulse and measured it at 130. His breathing was very shallow; his blood pressure had soared to 205/?130. They took him to the nearest emergency center, Lakefield General.

When the ambulance arrived, Bruce was taken straight in and seen by the attending physician, who discovered that Bruce demonstrated the rigidity associated with severe brain injury when pain stimulation was applied. Bruce was comatose. These signs suggested there was a significant problem with Bruce's brain, so the doctor ordered a CT angiogram scan and asked the charge nurse to page the on-call neurologist.

In many hospitals the ER only has access to a regular CT scanner, but Lakefield's new Integrated Stroke Research and Care Center designation meant the attending physician could triage patients to the neurology wing and use the specialized equipment there. The doctor was fairly certain this patient had a serious brain injury, possibly because of a stroke, and if so, a CT angiogram would be of great benefit. By this time Bruce had had a blockage in his brain for about four hours.

Shortly after Bruce's CT angiogram was conducted in the neurology wing, Eli Pattern was able to make a specific diagnosis of stroke for Bruce.

Dr. Pattern could see that the patient was in an advanced stage of carotid stenosis, which meant that the blood vessels in his neck were narrowed as a result of a buildup of plaque. The plaque formed as result of blood clots, calcium, and cholesterol deposits. Carotid stenosis is difficult to pick up in a general examination. A physician can detect it if they specifically examine the arteries in the neck, and then hear or see reduced blood flow; otherwise, the most common way for it to be discovered is through an ultrasound examination of the carotid artery or, as in this case, once it is too late and the patient has already had a stroke. The carotid arteries are the primary blood vessels feeding the brain, so a reduction or blockage is a critical situation.

The scan showed that the patient had blockages in two separate areas, in both the left and right sides of his brain. First, Dr. Pattern had seen that there was high-grade stenosis, or severe narrowing, at the branching region of the right middle cerebral artery (MCA) trunk, suggesting it was blocked by a blood clot, which could be treated.

Second, on Bruce's left side he had an obstruction of his internal carotid artery, affecting the network of arteries called the circle of Willis, as well as the anterior communicating artery, which joins the left and right cerebral arteries at the front of the brain. Because there was limited blood flow from the other hemisphere because of the blockage in the MCA, Dr. Pattern was concerned that other areas were going to be significantly affected.[12] Internal carotid artery concerns on the left side suggested that similar problems were occurring on the right internal carotid artery; getting Bruce into magnetic resonance imaging would help examine these effects and measure the volume of blood flow throughout the brain.

The bigger question for Dr. Pattern, though, was determining a course of action to manage Bruce's blockages; he needed to act fast. Pattern didn't know how long Bruce had been experiencing this ischemic event. Even if he could effect some positive changes, what would the result for the patient be, if he even survived? Though often unspoken by physicians, they sometimes let severe cases, like this patient's, evolve on their own because to attempt treatment at such a late stage of a traumatic event, particularly when it involved the brain, often meant creating a long drawn out death or a long period of profound disability. In these extreme cases sometimes it was best to let it run its course.

Dr. Pattern did not have any contact information for the next of kin yet—Bruce had been brought in with no identification on him—so he was left to his own devices as to how to proceed. He was already aware that Bruce's prognosis was poor based on his admission values, such as his blood pressure and heart rate, as well his Glasgow Coma Scale score of three out of 15, indicating deep unconsciousness.

Dr. Pattern decided to go with his training; he believed it was essential to begin intravenous thrombolysis to dissolve blood clots using a recombinant tissue plasminogen activator (r-tPA).[13,14] There were, however, concerns about the timing: according to US and Canadian guidelines, clot-dissolving thrombolytic drugs should be given within three hours of a stroke-related event. But in Europe the thrombolytic drug alteplase had been approved for use within four and a half hours of the event.[14] Pattern felt it was the best chance to restore function for Bruce.

There was a downside of applying this treatment, though, namely that Bruce could bleed to death from a brain hemorrhage as blood flow was restored to his injured brain tissue. But Dr. Pattern believed this was the best course of action despite the glaring risk factor of Bruce's very high blood pressure. He believed surgery would be pointless now and would most likely lead to the patient's death.

Bruce was transferred to the dedicated imaging suite to monitor the effects of r-tPA therapy. Dr. Pattern would look for blood flow returning to the affected regions and would keep a close watch for bleeding in the brain caused by the medication. Pattern's only other course of action for Bruce, should further blockages occur, would be to give him an antithrombotic or anticoagulant drug, such as heparin, to prevent more clots from forming. He decided, however, that he would begin treatment and monitor the man's condition via the intensive care unit and act as needed. But the prognosis did not look good.

CHAPTER 5
DECLAN

"Detective! Detective, are you listening?" said the man across the table. My newest informant, Norman, was an elderly gentleman who lived in one of our "targeted" buildings in the district. Truth be told, I was not listening. I was busy in my happy place, which I liked to drift to these days since I was getting close to retirement. I did have trouble listening sometimes, especially to individuals who were more detached than attached when it came to reality.

Though Norman had given us some good information the first time we met, on the last three occasions the information turned out to be nothing and today he seemed to be exceptionally... detached, thus my lack of attention. I forced myself to focus. "Of course I'm listening, I'm always listening." In my line of work listening was a good idea; you never knew when you were going to get that little piece of information that made a difference. After all, the "Son of Sam" serial killer was caught as a result of a parking ticket, which is a good lesson for a police department and one I like to bring up when I talk to new recruits.

After about forty minutes, though, I called this meeting to a close. I stood. "Okay. Thanks for the info, Norman, as always." His comments today had included details about such things as "cold war style" secret agents, though I was unsure what he meant by that. Was their clothing from the 1950s, or did they talk a certain way? Perhaps they carried very large "secret" equipment? He'd also given me a description of a prostitution ring run out of an apartment two floors below his, as well as a possible meth lab operating in the penthouse of the building. Again, though Norman was a bit... all over the place, he was retired and he sat in the lobby for a good part of the day, so he saw a lot of people coming and going.

"I know I can always count on you to let us know when everybody's coming and going. It's helpful, Norman." Especially when it came to corroboration for search warrant applications. So to keep Norman motivated we needed to meet with him from time to time, and that included listening to all his theories, which included not only crime problems in his building but also his ideas on how the city could improve its services. Oh, the joys of the general investigation division. I shook his hand and headed for my car.

I had transferred back to general investigation less than a year ago from the homicide cold case unit, which had been my world for the better part of six and a half years. I thoroughly enjoyed examining cold files because there was no better feeling than finding that one detail that could break a case. But that goes with a significant amount of frustration in reviewing files for weeks and finding nothing of importance, which happens with the majority of the cases, usually because there was simply very little information at all. During my time in the unit, though, I had been successful in getting convictions in two cases and solving one other very long-term case. To an outsider that might not seem like a great record, but in the cold case unit it was quite remarkable.

One of those cases had seen no movement and no new information for twenty-one years, until I was assigned to it and started the review.

The case involved the murder of a teenage girl working the night shift at a local chain restaurant. It appeared that at closing time, she had let someone into the restaurant. Cash was missing from the cash trays and the safe had been damaged but not breached. There appeared to have been no struggle. From this information, it seemed the girl knew the assailant and that robbery was the motive. As a cold case detective your job is to stand back and review the evidence with an open mind, review the direction of the original investigation, and try to find anomalies.

The key is to take your time. I examined every piece of evidence, taking nothing for granted. A fresh pair of eyes may notice something that might have been viewed as normal originally, but might be out of place. In this case, that something was a children's toy, part of a promotional giveaway, found on the floor near the body.

I had this toy on my desk for weeks after bringing it up from the evidence room. One day, I searched the internet to see if it was collectable. But I discovered something else. Investigators had thought nothing of it originally because there was a whole box of these toys nearby. But they hadn't noticed that this toy was just a little different from the ones in the box. The toys in the box were the same as those given out nation-wide, but the slightly different type on the floor had been provided to only three stores in the country.

Investigators had suspected a former boyfriend of the victim, who worked at the same restaurant chain but at a location across town. But there was nothing to link him to the crime, until now: the store the ex-boyfriend worked at was one of the three that had received the slightly different toy; the other two were thousands of miles away. With diligence, I found the dates of the toy promotion and discovered that the toys at the boyfriend's store had been delivered only the day before the murder, suggesting that only someone who had worked at that store the day before could have had one of the toys. And the boyfriend had indeed worked the day the toys were delivered. But he had an alibi: his mother said that at the time of the murder, he had been home with her watching a movie. I was beginning to wonder about that.

The original interview with the mother had been short because the motive appeared to be robbery and the ex-boyfriend didn't fit that theory. This time we pressed a little harder and she admitted that her son had gone out for a while, but she insisted he was not gone long—he had just run to the store and was home for most of the movie, since he saw the beginning and the end. But it turned out the movie they had watched was *JFK*, which is over three hours long.

A new interview of the victim's best friend revealed that the former boyfriend had been upset when they broke up and had fought with one of the victim's male friends when he saw them walking home from school together two days before the murder. This new information helped establish a motive. The friend said she hadn't mentioned this to the police before because she didn't think it was important. But it was another piece to the puzzle, one that meant we could bring the boyfriend in for new questioning. We believed we could take a run at him. I was voted the one most likely to break him down.

I had done my homework on the suspect's life since the murder. There had been a lot of failures for this individual and several interactions with the police, including domestic assaults and bar fights—clear signs of anger management problems.

I set the interview for late afternoon, ensuring it would go over the dinner hour. For the first hour we merely chatted, barely mentioning the case. I was trying to develop respect and trust between us, letting him know I was his friend. I offered to get him something to eat, which would help build a bond while we waited for the food, but the truth was, it was never coming.

Finally, I begin to talk about the case. He had spoken with his mother recently, of course, and was aware that we now knew he had not been home all night, so he had had time to develop a story. He said he had gone to the convenience store down the street, bought some food, and hung out in the parking lot eating his snack before going home. Conveniently, no one else had been around. I took time making pointless notes, allowing uncertainty to build in his mind. Then I hit him with some critical but not quite truthful information. But because we had developed trust, he would believe me.

I told him the bank across the street had a security camera that showed the convince store parking lot. I told him the bank archived its security footage, by date, for twenty-five years. He appeared surprised by this. I said that while we were talking, detectives were checking the footage so we could put suspicion to rest. I asked what time he had been at the store. He became flustered and claimed he couldn't remember. After that he didn't say much. I told him that once we checked that night's footage, we should be all done.

I left the interview room, watching him on camera while I had some dinner. I went back in and hit him with the information about the fight two days before the murder, something he did not know we were aware of. I commiserated with him about how passionate we can get about someone we love.

Four hours after we started, I finally hit him with the information about the toy. I then said I knew he was lying about being at the convenience store because the footage did not show him there, and he finally broke down. He began to cry and I could tell he wanted to tell his story. He wanted someone to know he had made a terrible mistake and he was looking for forgiveness, for understanding, and he found that in me—in addition to the cameras and microphones rolling in the interview room.

This moment is very important for an investigator, and a good one knows when to say nothing and just wait, which is what I did. Finally, with a big sigh, he began to speak. He explained how he went to the restaurant to tell her he loved her and wanted her back, but she wouldn't listen. This made him angry. "I don't know what happened next. I kinda just blacked out and the next thing I knew she was on the floor, blood spilling out of her, and I was holding a bloody knife." He grabbed the cash to make it look like robbery, also scratching at the safe. He ran out of the store to a bridge three streets south to throw the knife into the river. At home, he stuck his bloody shirt in the garage, went in the back door, saying to his mom that he was going upstairs to change into his PJs. He watched the rest of the movie in a daze.

When I asked about the toy, he said he had grabbed it during his shift the day before because he thought it was cool, and he hadn't realized he had lost it until today. He had forgotten all about it. But that small thing was the key that let me break a twenty-year-old case. Sometimes the simplest thing can trip a person up.

The department rewarded me for my efforts with an extra day off and a piece of paper telling me "good work." But that never really mattered to me; more important was that I brought peace to a family that had been wondering all these years who had killed their daughter, and that's something no one can put a value on. It's the best feeling in the world for me—nothing can compare.

But cases like that take so much out of you that your personal life can really suffer. Though they can be rewarding, in the end these cases are emotionally draining for an investigator, and you wonder how you can possibly start another one. Nevertheless, on your desk the next day is a new file and another person's afterlife in your hands. It is a heavy responsibility.

Though I enjoyed that work immensely it was time for a change, and I headed back to the general investigation office of my old district. It felt like home. General investigations included any crime you could think of: break and enter, thefts, assaults, frauds—basically everything not handled by our specialized units, such as homicide, drugs or hold-up. I was back in the thick of it.

The job meant we spent a lot of time sitting writing up cases for prosecutors and ensuring all the paperwork was in place and prepared for court. Court was another place we spent a lot of our time, often on days we weren't actually at work, which meant we worked all the time, basically.

When I was in the office, I had no time to go out for a proper lunch, and though I can pack a healthy lunch, I don't always eat it. Instead, I get whatever the office is ordering in that day. You name it, we take it out: Thai, Chinese, Italian, Afghan, Iranian, and Greek, not to mention the fusion restaurants we began ordering from. Nothing like a good noodle burger to keep your taste buds alive. When I was younger, I could eat and eat and never worry about my weight or my health; I had no issues. No reflux, no heartburn, no cholesterol problem. Okay, I never had it checked. But I was sure it was good; I felt great, well ok.

For a young guy on the job health was just something you took for granted. But lately I'd been getting the same advice from my physician (because I actually started going): "You need to stay healthy, watch what you eat, and be careful not to add extra pounds because as you age it is going to be more difficult to take them off."

The past few months I had been at my heaviest, but by no means did I consider myself obese. I was just starting to build a well-earned stomach, which many of my friends had already had for a while. Though I had always believed that being in policing meant it was essential to stay in shape, because when the fight is on you need to be ready, when I was in the cold case division I was not out of the office much investigating fresh scenes, so my expectation of having to chase or fight anyone was slim to none. But now that I was back in general investigations and would be traveling to crime scenes, I felt it was a good time to take off a bit of weight, for several reasons.

Like any good investigator I did a little research. One thing I found out about weight gain and aging is that generally, the two are not a good combination, especially if you would like to live a long life. Surprise! Which made me wonder how many really obese individuals reach the age of eighty. I turned to the internet to get an idea of how being overweight might affect my health in the years to come. I steered clear of pop culture sites and I turned to more academic sites to get a true estimate of what I was in for.

What I found was not surprising in some respects. Being even just somewhat overweight was related to many health problems, and the effects compound as we age.

One thing I found surprising was that as an aging male, if I was overweight I had a significant risk of stroke. I read that just a slight increase in my body mass index could result in a 6% increase in my risk for stroke.[15-18] I knew that being overweight could cause problems, but as I read further I also found that this increased risk for stroke existed even without high blood pressure, diabetes, or high cholesterol levels.[17,18]

This makes sense, though: the brain is a vascular organ, so what affects the body must affect the brain too. This made me think that maybe conditions that affect the heart might also affect the brain. And sure enough, with another search I found some research that showed exactly that. This research referred to a condition called atrial fibrillation (A-fib). As describe by the Heart and Stroke Foundation, A-fib is a condition in which the heart beats irregularly. A-fib risk increases as you age, and the major concern with A-fib is that it is related to strokes. In fact, research has shown that if an individual has A-fib the risk of stroke can increases three to five times that of the general population.[19]

After I read that, I was quick to check the symptoms list, which included rapid heartbeat; chest pain or pressure; shortness of breath, especially during exertion or anxiety; fatigue; dizziness; sweating; and light-headedness.[20] I tried to remember if I'd experienced any of those symptoms recently, then wondered if I was an internet hypochondriac.

Deep in thought, I missed the fact that the other shift had come in. My partner had already left for the night and the other detective was on his way out too. "Are you staying, or do you want to go get a drink?" he asked just before he reached the door.

I thought about it only briefly. "Maybe just a quick one." My research faded from my mind as my computer screen went dark. I grabbed my jacket and headed out the door.

***

I got into work the next day just before 8:00 AM. We usually work twelve-hour shifts, depending on what occurs during a given shift; sometimes it can be much longer. It was Sunday so I was hoping for a slower day, because that quick drink with the guys last night had turned into eight or ten, followed by a stop for a burger and fries, with a side of onion rings. Oh boy. I longed to be young again. No worries, I promised myself for the 168th time; next time I'll take it easy.

At about 9:00am on Sundays the detective staff and patrol sergeants get together to review the week's cases and clear the air of any issues that arose over the past week. The Sunday meeting always takes place over breakfast, which means a trip to our local diner. We were regulars there because the food was cheap and good.

Sunday breakfast was one of my favorite meals of the week. I order my usual steak and eggs with an extra-large severing of hash browns and topped it off with a large coffee, double cream, double sugar. As we ate, we reviewed the week's cases, relaying our progress on ongoing investigations and the results of the arrests over the past week. I passed along the information I had received from Norman this week to make sure they were aware of it and to see what they thought. After breakfast we headed back to the office, but not before I got one more doubled-up coffee to go. Maybe when I get back to the office, I thought, I should look up the effects of so much coffee. I was fairly certain what the result would be, especially with the double additives.

Sunday at the office was usually a paperwork day. Though busy times were unpredictable, the busiest times were generally Fridays and Saturdays. It seems that when individuals have too much time on their hands, and are in close proximity to other people who have too much time on their hands, the result is contact with the police. Sunday was the day we usually counted on to complete our files for upcoming court cases, to tie up any loose ends, and to complete our bail compliance checks and reports.

Every district had a number of higher-risk individuals who were either under house arrest or on probation and were required to be at home on certain days of the week or by certain times. We had a few under house arrest and a few who had to be in their residences over the weekend and were only permitted to travel to work and back through the week.

First thing Sunday morning was a good time to check compliance because often people under house arrest who liked to sneak out to party Saturday nights did not always make it home till later the next day, thereby breaching their conditions. To ensure the public was safe, we liked to catch them before they even went out, but the reality of policing was that we seemed to have evolved into a reactive element—there were just too many offences creating too many calls to handle with too few resources. So sometimes we ended up reacting to events after the fact, rather than being proactive and preventive in our approach. Today, my partner, Abigail, and I were going to try to do a little of both.

Abigail was a new detective who had arrived in the office only a couple of weeks before and so I was trying to show her the ropes. She seemed very tenacious, refusing to let anything go, especially when it came to criminals. She would find a way to get the job done. Abigail had shoulder-length brown hair, piercing blue eyes, and a quick wit, which is a refreshing change in our department. She was a competitive triathlete, something I used to be, so we could talk about running, biking, and swimming quite a lot.

Abigail had a university degree in forensic psychology with a minor in computer science, which was part of the reason I chose her as a partner: she knows so much more than I do, and I have learned that it's a good idea to surround yourself with people who can do things you can't. Her fresh knowledge was a great resource.

One of our compliance checks today was on a guy named Tony. Tony was out of jail and on probation for his fifth drug trafficking offence, which was apparently a family business, and he couldn't seem to do anything but sell drugs. I took a special interest in the case because Tony had no limits on who he would sell drugs to; he just didn't care. As a result, we had seen a recent rise in overdoses in the area, especially among high school students. But we had not been able to catch him in the act this time.

Today I was hoping things might be different because we'd gotten a tip from our drug squad that led us to believe Tony might be getting a visit from a regular customer needing a quick fix, at around 11:00 AM, the earliest Tony would do business, we knew. We arrived about 10:35. I set myself up in an unmarked car across the street and to the left of Tony's front door, pretending I was texting, though I was actually recording. Abigail was at the bus stop to the right of the house. The plan was to grab the buyer after the exchange, confirm Tony had sold him drugs, and then move in for a "compliance check," after which we would calmly cuff him and explain why he was under arrest.

We didn't have to wait long. Our user arrived and knocked on the window to the right of the door. Tony came to the door and an exchange was made just inside the open front door.

As the user crossed the street, Abigail followed. As they passed me, I got out of the car and followed them. Just as we were out of sight of the house, we asked him to stop. He turned, and I saw a familiar look in his eyes: we were in for a chase. Not too smart, I thought, smiling. Abigail had completed a 10 km run the week before in forty-six minutes, and that is very quick. The user ran, and the chase was on; he cut between two houses with Abigail close behind. I headed to the top of the street, huffing and puffing almost immediately. They were running through yards, climbing fences, and jumping shrubbery.

I called for the patrol car we had on standby to head north four streets and told the officers to get out and head south looking for the foot chase. I was still moving at a reasonable pace, but before I'd gone another block I heard over the radio that Abigail had him; nice work, I thought. As I rounded the corner, I saw the patrol officers searching the suspect. They located an eight-ball of cocaine and one joint, which was all we needed. It didn't take long for the user to give up his dealer because he knew we would cut him loose if he gave us a sworn statement right there. We had also used the patrol car camera to record the suspect describing the transaction we had just seen.

Instead of simply arresting Tony, we decided to get a search warrant too. I thought this would be great experience for Abigail. After a few minutes' chase and Abigail's capture, we were in for a few hours of paperwork getting our warrant together, and then more paperwork after we brought Tony in.

I was lamenting the paperwork because I wanted to get out early today and go for a run, inspired by Abigail's performance. I needed to get back to running before I got too sedentary. But now I had to sit down for a few hours with this case. That reminded me that I had heard something about sitting being as bad for your health as smoking. Hmm... maybe I should look that up when I get home, right after I get that workout in.

Twenty minutes before the end of our shift, just as we were completing our case notes for the day, including the write-up of Tony's arrest, which had netted half a kilo of cocaine and a handgun, we got a call about a house explosion at the northwest end of our district. Fire and patrol officers were on scene. I really did not want to work for another six hours today.

I asked the detectives coming in for the next shift if they could do a quick assessment and hold the scene for me and I would go out first thing tomorrow to investigate. Abigail had booked the day off tomorrow, so it would just be me. Our team was really good, and they agreed. Thank heavens.

As soon as I got home, I hit the treadmill hard and ran a good distance more than I had in years. It was struggle, but I had to do it. My breathing was very labored and my chest was heaving, but I got it done. I promised myself I'd keep it going; I'd get another run in tomorrow, and I'd make sure I changed my eating so I could drop this excess weight. Goodbye, steak and eggs. I had a bit of a headache as I got ready for bed, but I wasn't surprised, after the run, and I was certain it would go away after I rehydrated.

I got to the district for my Monday shift about 9:00 AM. On the board from yesterday was the explosion and fire scene that required further examination today. After a quick look last night, the scene had been held for a better examination today.

The detective going off duty brought me up to speed. "We're not sure how the fire started, other than that it was the result of a large explosion, epic in fact. Once the fire was out, Fire found a body in the rubble. No ID available at this point. Lucky you—your shift, your investigation!" He laughed as he headed out the door.

The Fire Marshal's office would be taking the lead in the investigation of the fire, but we still needed to identify the body and have an autopsy completed to determine whether the fire or the explosion had been the cause of death, or something else. I was planning to meet with the Fire Marshal's office at 2:00 PM. The coroner had already left me a message this morning, indicating that it looked like the explosion was the major contributing factor in the death, having caused significant trauma to the internal organs and blunt force trauma to the back of the head.

I still planned to attend the scene today because there were a number of unanswered questions. For one, the cause of the explosion was still to be determined. Normally I would leave it to the Fire Marshal's office but since the victim was still unidentified, we ran the address to help ID the individual. Though normally it is fairly easy to get the required information with a phone call, this house was listed under a corporation's name and determining the actual resident was becoming a challenge. Neighbors had said they never saw the resident of the house, but the lawn was always well maintained by a service and if people came to the house it was often late at night, so they assumed the person living there must be a night worker.

To us, though, this information, the difficulty locating an owner, and the fact that there was an explosion might suggest there was a drug lab being operated in this home; hence the interest from my department.

At 12:30 PM I arrived at the scene to survey the damage; it was quite remarkable. The explosion was so powerful that half of the right front corner of the home to the left of the burned house had collapsed—it was so bad the residents had difficulty getting out of their front door. Fortunately, there were no injuries in that home. The home to the right of the house that exploded had pieces of wood and siding embedded in it, to the extent that some sections of siding had penetrated the home. These homeowners had been asleep when the explosion occurred and a piece of siding had come through their bedroom wall just above their heads, giving them a wakeup call they had not expected. People three blocks away were finding debris in their yards. It was an amazing scene. You could not even really tell that a house had stood there. It looked like just a pile of rubble. Household articles, wood, plaster, and insulation were all over the street and in nearby tress. It was like a war zone.

We had blocked off both ends of the street and there were officers keeping pedestrians and homeowners from approaching the scene or entering potentially unsafe nearby homes. There was, of course, a constant stream of individuals who wanted to get a look at rubble. Crazy what people find interesting.

I could see a number of forensic officers milling around, trying to plot the location of the explosion and provide an accurate description of what occurred and where. They were also taking samples amid the rubble to help identify the type of explosive material that had created this disaster. I had asked another patrol car to attend the scene with me, as I wanted assistance gathering information related to who the victim might have been and to determine whether there might be connections to organized crime. I gathered the team together to give them instructions related to locating computer hard drives, cellphone SIM cards, and any paper that may have information we could use. I realized at that moment I had a splitting headache and would need to grab a Tylenol from the car when I was finished.

As I began to speak, odd looks came to my colleagues' faces.

PART II

A NEW PERCEPTIVE

Chapter 6

Declan

After I woke up, I spent the first few minutes analyzing last night's dream, which involved being wrapped in bandages by paramedics from the top of my head to the tip of my toes and then being placed in a coroner's bag. I couldn't move—similar to the effects of the stroke, I guess.

It was a very disturbing dream, similar to waking dreams I'd had where I think I'm paralyzed. I found those events disturbing enough that I looked the phenomenon up. I discovered that this happened to lots of people. Apparently, what happens is that the area in your brain that activates conscious muscle movement is still asleep, so you are temporarily paralyzed; you're aware, but cannot move. Luckily, it lasts only very briefly.

When it happened to me, regardless of the time of night I would always get up and make sure I could still walk and move around. And then I would always ensure I had no covers near my face and that my head was nice and high on my pillow, so that just in case I *did* become paralyzed I would be able to breathe. So now, just in case I slipped back into sleep, I maneuvered myself higher up on my pillow.

I did feel much better today, though. I tested my limbs and discovered I had more feeling on my right side and I was beginning to be able to move it, however slowly. But even that was so much better than yesterday.

I glanced around my hospital room. It was very early in the morning. The others appeared to be sleeping, including the visitor of the woman beside me, so I didn't have to worry about looking like an idiot "Hello?" I said quietly, listening carefully to the result. "Can you hear me now?" A little slurred and sloppy, but reasonable. It seemed I had my speech back, for the most part.

What an improvement over the course of a day and half. I was able to sit up almost on my own and I would be able to complain about the food, as well as the cups of ice and the tiny straws. I found it remarkable that I could have been in such bad shape less than forty-eight hours ago. My improvement seemed almost miracle-like.

Sarah, the nurse, came in. "Dr. White will be in to check on you later. I can see you're feeling much better."

"And sounding better, I hope," I said slowly.

"Definitely! Good work!" I didn't recall doing any work, but I was happy to take credit. Sarah checked all the machines in the room and continued on her way. If I was really that much better, I was going to advocate for leaving intensive care today, and maybe even go home. I felt I did not need to be taking up a space here any longer and I certainly knew that hospitals liked to free up beds. However, I had a feeling that physicians also liked to keep their patients alive and so sometimes had to fight administration to keep the patient in the bed. But I hoped this was not going to be the case for me.

To my right, the woman's visitor had fallen asleep with her head on the woman's lap, so I assumed they were quite close. I had not seen that patient awake. The two men opposite were asleep too, though I had seen one of them, the one with the quilt, sitting up and talking; he seemed to be doing well. The other, like the woman, I had never seen awake. It didn't give me a good feeling.

I wanted to know how much I could do. I could move my right leg but I wasn't sure it would actually support me. My first goal was to check my legs to see if they worked before alerting the nurse that I wanted to get up; there was no point in doing that if I couldn't actually move. Trying to be as quiet as possible, I shifted so I was sitting on the left edge of my bed, where my IV was securely tied, in addition to monitors that were connected to me, which I knew would begin beeping if I disconnected them.

Planting my feet flat and far enough apart to keep me steady, I held the bedrail and stood. So far, so good. After standing for a few moments I was fairly certain I should be able to walk, so I pushed the call button to get a little assistance. Sarah returned quite promptly. I could get used to this.

"I want to get out of the room and go for a bit of a walk," I whispered.

I assumed I was going to have to engage in a whispered argument with her about my need to get out of here for a bit, but she just whispered back, "No problem, Detective Myles. Just give me a minute to fix this so we can make you mobile." She moved with quiet haste, detaching two monitors and untying the IV stand, and in a moment I was free. She helped me to the hallway, guiding my IV pole.

"Thank you," I said carefully, slowly. "I'm grateful to get up and move around. I thought hospitals were keen on keeping people in their beds, especially... wobbly people, because they're concerned about us falling and suing the hospital."

Sarah laughed. "Not to worry, Detective Myles. We have some good lawyers here." She kept a firm grip on my elbow as I shuffled along. "And this wing is different—

different from other hospitals and even from other wings in this hospital. Our goal is to get people active and interactive and you certainly can't do that sitting alone in a hospital bed, can you?"

"No, I'd say not." I still had to make a specific effort to form each word.

"Because of our new Integrated Stroke Research and Care Center designation, we've been able to create a dedicated wing that's actually staffed at the proper numbers, which virtually never happens, so we have enough nurses to assist with patients' needs. And we can get you out of your room when you want." She relaxed her grip a little, letting me take steps more or less on my own.

"Our goal is to get you back to one hundred percent; that's what we strive for. And one of the best ways to do that is to get you up and active. A lot of the research we try to act on here indicates that exercise is beneficial for so many things, so we really don't want to restrict your movement, unless you're a danger to yourself—and you seem to be doing fine. In fact, stroke patients are usually more apprehensive about their abilities than they need to be; they can do more than they think they can. When someone wants to walk, let them walk, is our motto." With that, she let go of my arm, but stayed close. "As well, the brain is a vascular organ and it's fed by rich oxygenated blood, and what better way to get the blood flowing than to move around." She stopped and gave me a very gentle, good-natured nudge, indicating that I was free to go on my own.

I smiled and "took off" down the hall, thinking that whoever is in charge here is definitely on the right track. I realized my ass was on display at the back of my hospital gown. I didn't care.

It was great to be up and about. My right side still had some tingles, a pins-and-needles feeling, but it was working okay and I was able to walk fairly well, if slowly and cautiously. I wondered if some of the weakness, and a little dizziness, was just related to the fact that I had been in bed for a couple of days and my legs were just getting used to moving again. As I walked down the hall, in various rooms I could see patients working with staff on all sorts of activities.

One room was labeled Games Room. I was expecting some sedate board games stacked in the corner with a few tables and folding chairs. What I saw when I paused in the doorway, however, was anything but sedate. The room had a number of posters on the wall, lots of colour—and a bunch of big standalone arcade games, the kind you would have seen in any arcade in the early eighties. There was also a pinball machine, a foosball table, table tennis, and air hockey! Was this a hospital or a resort? The room clearly wasn't reserved for staff breaks because there were a couple of patients in there playing with the machines, some with monitors on poles at their sides, with staff members looking on. If this was therapy, sign me up.

Farther down the hall was what looked like a traditional physiotherapy room, with whirlpools, a wading pool, staircases, bars to hold while walking, and treadmills with tether systems hanging from the ceiling to support the patient. Again, patients were working away, supported by attentive staff.

At the end of the hall was a set of four plain double doors. Above them was a sign: Mae's Auditorium. I wondered briefly about Mae and why the auditorium was named for her. On the wall to the right of the doors was a glassed-covered board announcing weekly lectures. Today's lecture was by Dr. Evelyn White: Stroke Rehabilitation: What We Have Learned and What We Can Do; 6:50 AM. I didn't know what time it was but I could hear through the doors that the lecture in progress. I opened one door an inch, and through the crack I could see Dr. White speaking.

I opened the door, slipped into the lecture hall, and sat in the back row. On the screen behind Dr. White was a large image of a brain's inner anatomy. The image's label indicated it was the interior blood vessels of an adult brain. It made me think that I had seen brains far too often and they never looked like this. The lecture hall could hold, I would guess, around 300 people and it was about one-third full, which I thought was remarkable for an early morning lecture.

There were a lot of short white coats in the audience, though, suggesting that many medical students were in attendance—maybe it was mandatory, which explained the large turnout. I always figured people had to have a motive. Maybe that's why I had done well as a detective but not in relationships—I was always looking for the angle. The students in the audience looked so young I almost wondered if they let high school classes attend. I smiled when I remembered how my daughter often reminded me that I was old and out of touch.

Dr. White was wrapping up her point about the structure of the brain and its vessels, luckily for me, or I would have been lost for a while. She was now beginning to talk about the Stroke Center here at the hospital.

"As a designated Integrated Stroke Research and Care Center," she explained, "there's a significant research component involved in all aspects of the care we provide.

The unit's philosophy is to place great emphasis on evidence-based research strategies and to apply these clinically to the stroke program and track both long- and short-term changes in our patient populations. The benefit of having a guiding and fluid program is just that: we have a program and guidelines based on the best evidence and best-practice results. These programs are also fluid because our surgeons, physicians, other clinicians, and researchers are constantly monitoring the evolution of stroke care and they're open to modifying our program as needed. This only works when you have a dedicated team of individuals all open to change and willing to meet regularly to stay on top of the evolving literature, and to then apply proven information whenever possible in a treatment program, as recommended by the clinical research team. Thus, this is a teaching/learning unit where we foster a new level of interaction between our researchers and our clinicians. In some cases, they are one and the same, which makes for a very effective team member.

"This type of movement in medicine is sorely needed and I believe history will show this as a real turning point. You might remember," she continued, "from your History of Medicine course that lobotomies and psychosurgery were performed routinely from about the 1930s well into the 1960s[21] in the belief that a great benefit was being provided to the patient—but with little thought about its consequences. If we were to suggest such an application today, the response would either be laughter or shock. Maybe both.

"One must remember that changing even the simplest thing in a hospital, or in any healthcare setting, is very difficult. For example, for literally centuries in the Western world, hospitals believed that keeping the family away from the patient was the best approach because it would give the patient time to rest and recover. But clinical research now clearly tells us we need to open the doors to patients' families. They need to see their loved ones, and when they do, the patient's health improves. Another reason for restricting access in the past was that it makes it easier to keep patients in a routine, helping healthcare staff manage a floor or a ward. This can be done more easily with fewer distractions, and that has historically been argued as translating into better care for patients. As well, the understanding of infectious processes in the environment was limited many decades ago, and since hospitals were unsure of how to effectively reduce infection, one easy way was to limited access to the hospital."

I wanted to hear this so I stayed, idly wondering if anyone was wondering where I was. Dr. White continued. "At Lakefield General's Stroke Center, we base decisions on the evolving research in healthcare and stroke care, which includes encouraging family members to come to the unit. In fact, we have asked staff to use family members to their advantage and make them part of the care plan. And it's worked out really well, because with family around, if, for example, the patient is thirsty or needs to sit up in the bed, get to the washroom, whatever, then it's really helpful to have a family member present to assist with this care, and it frees up our team to focus on other elements of their care or to help other patients. It also gets family members accustomed to performing this sort of care because in some cases they have to continue it at home.

"Another old argument was that the patient is in our care and if something should happen to them while a family member, rather than a staff member, is assisting them, then the hospital is liable. But we apply common sense. The care plan is available for everyone, including the family, to see at the head of each bed and it indicates if assistance is required for mobility and if so, they're asked to summon a staff member. We communicate that verbally as well.

"Another bonus is that sometimes, the hospital staff has trouble communicating with patients for a number of reasons—language barrier, speech patterns—and when family members are present these interactions become a lot easier. I'm sure you know how to translate that particular look your mother gives you, or your father's grunt, into a defined need better than our staff. So we want the help and the patients need the help, so why not use it?"

Made sense to me. Dr. White continued. "The idea of isolating the patient is, in my opinion, nonsense, and as such we've changed this process for our patient population and encourage families to be by their side, even in the ICU, whenever possible. With this simple change in policy—a simple change in traditional thought, really—we have had significant improvement in the health of our patients and have improved their hospital experience. We have reduced the length of stay in the hospital for many of these patients, freeing up room and helping us treat as many as possible. We're all quite aware that the administration's goal is to free up beds; it's part of their job and it's understandable, but that is not the goal of the Stroke Center or the goal for better care."

Dr. White paused to take a sip of water and then continued. "In some cases, we have been able to improve patient performance by increasing the duration of the hospital stay. For many of these individuals we provide a more comprehensive treatment program. What this does is that it helps us ensure there are fewer return visits to the hospital for these patients. The research shows that if we hold on to the right patients a bit longer and treat them better, they experience fewer adverse events post discharge. This concept, again, is based on best evidence and when applied effectively it works, with the proper components in place. So in the long term we are again reducing the need for further healthcare intervention down the road and reducing the strain on the healthcare system overall. Discharging patients too early increases their chance of re-admission, which has been shown in a number of studies. This isn't just stroke patients but all patients."

She posted on the screen the abstract of a 2012 study by the Canadian Institute for Health Information. She read, "The risk of re-admission increased by around 40% in patients discharged from hospitals with an average length of stay that was more than one day shorter than the national average expected length of stay."[22,23] Showing the next slide, Dr. White said, "In 2013, researchers reported that on average, the cost of stroke hospitalization (in 2010) was about $21 million in the United States, and that about 20–40% of these patients were re-admitted within a year of first admission. They also highlighted that 25% of these re-admissions occurred within a month of the initial admission.[24] One of the major factors contributing to re-admission was the lack of follow-up health services, as well as the worsening of residual stroke symptoms.[24] This would suggest to us as researchers that the initial difficulties with stroke are not being treated to the extent that would allow for the success of the patient when discharged from the hospital."

I drifted off in my own head and wondered if hospitals have this information and they're aware of the significant cost of re-admissions, then why would hospitals not put in place more comprehensive programs to reduce re-admissions? Why not help patients and families so they don't end up back in here?

When Dr. White continued, she explained that "the 2013 article I mentioned suggested that one of the major problems related to re-admission was a result of the 'medical management' of patients during their hospital stay, which has been shown to be preventable with the proper care and focused attention on the patient's needs.[24] Some of you are no doubt wondering, if we have all this information, and we could put more resources toward the care of the patients and focus on these preventable problems, why we aren't doing this, especially because this is in patients' best interests." She paused with her arms outstretched and a rehearsed look of puzzlement on her face?

At this moment I was also wondering if Dr. White was a mind reader, but I was also eager to hear her answer, so I didn't linger on this thought.

"In addition to the evidence I've already highlighted I would also like to point out that this type of program will also reduce the overall cost and perhaps lessen the strain on the healthcare system. So why are we not implementing these programs everywhere?"

She paused again to gather her thoughts. I got the impression she was making an effort to express the next point as tactfully as possible. "There are a couple of reasons. First, as I noted earlier, the way hospitals were historically, and are currently, structured, is a great impediment to change. Hospitals employ physicians who are trained to identify underlying problems, and once the problem has been identified it is then treated. Once it is treated the individual is ready to be discharged, which then makes room for another patient.

"That system allows us to treat as many patients as possible, as quickly as possible, rightly or wrongly, and is therefore the prevalent model in modern Western medicine. So similar to the way we have created fast food restaurants, we have created fast medicine. Notwithstanding the long wait times in some jurisdictions, of course.

"Second, and more likely the driving force behind the current model, is the way funding works for the care of patients in most countries and for most physicians. Once an individual is treated there is a cost for that treatment, including the initial diagnosis and the testing involved to discover the problem, which is often very costly. The funding formula related to the cost of diagnosing and treating an individual is normally front-end loaded and the longer the hospital stay, the smaller the ability to treat patients, with greater upfront costs. Short initial visits provide quick cash for hospitals and the quicker the treatment the more individuals can be ushered through the system. This type of care structure is short sighted and is not even a great business model because it doesn't take into account the secondary costs of improper treatment through return emergency room visits. It is a losing model for society, and a losing business model."

She held up her water bottle. "It's like buying a small bottle of water when you're thirsty; let's say it costs you a dollar. A bottle twice the size costs a dollar fifty. But you're not thinking about being thirsty later, you're just thinking about right now, so you get the small one. And that is sort of how our medical system works. They're not thinking about what will happen to that patient later, they're just interested in treating the problem at hand and moving the patient out as quickly as possible. So hospitals, clinics, and in some cases patients themselves just keep buying small bottles of water and the costs keep going up. When those patients return to the hospital, that's counted as a new visit and thus, congratulations!" she said with exaggerated enthusiasm. "We've treated another patient! When in fact you're retreating the same patient, but that's not how the funding model is set up. Each visit is a new case and your numbers reflect another treated individual."

I thought, wow, medical agencies—government or private, no matter what form—seem to have this dense bureaucracy that allows them to move forward at only a glacier's pace. I could feel my head starting to hurt and realized I longed to lie down again to get a little rest, but I really wanted to be a good student and stay to the end, so I remained in my seat.

Dr. White put up a slide showing the games room I had just passed. "Let's talk about stroke patients. If our stroke patients have experienced a significant brain injury, why do most hospitals focus mainly on the *physical* aspects of recovery? Certainly, we need to do more than ensure they can use the toilet or feed themselves before we release them. At Lakefield, we believe we need to retrain the organ that has been injured. If we work on training the brain, the physical aspects should follow. Brain training certainly assists in physical training. With this in mind, no pun intended," she added, "we have created stimulating environments for injured brains. The goal is to train people with brain injuries of any type as early as possible and as much as possible.

"We know that any brain at any age can grow neurons, and we also know from neuroscience researchers that stimulating environments with bright colours and differing activities and challenging novel tasks are effective for brain development and continued health.[25] For example, an individual who has experienced a stroke and may have a paralyzed limb, the goal, of course, is to get their paretic limb active, which typically is the goal of physical therapy sessions. However, what we need to remember is that the limb is controlled by the brain and fixing the brain will certainly assist in repairing external physical deficits. So we've created a dynamic environment full of different types of gaming activities.

"Surprisingly, one of the best ways we have found to assist with brain training is through the use of video games. If you haven't passed by our games room just down the hall from the auditorium, go have a look. We've got a bunch of video games consoles, so it's starting to look like an eighties arcade. Why arcade games? The effective use of visuomotor control is an integrated brain activity requiring the translation assistance of many brain areas to perform the tasks effectively. If you think of how we walk, talk, and navigate our environment, this is very similar to the tasks these games ask you to perform. There are also rules for performing tasks successfully, both in the real world and the virtual world.

"Note too that we are not limiting rehabilitation to these activities, we've added them to traditional therapy programs. We also have a bit of a shortage of physical, speech, and occupational therapists. So why not keep a room open and let the patients take charge of improving their performance on their own terms? It's a win for everyone. Our rehab games room is open 24/7—if a patient wants to use it at any time, they can. If the family wants to assist them to the room, that's great. The room's been open for over five months now and we track the hours that patients are in the room with an RFID tag in their hospital bracelet. These times in the room are added to research data and are available for all staff treating the individual. What I can tell you thus far is that there is a clear association between the hours spent in that room and increased improvement in a number of physical areas. In fact, I'd go so far as to say it's revolutionary for the care and continued success of these patients. We also compare this data with control patients with similar damage who haven't used the room. We can certainly tell you that month over month this hospital is outperforming traditional stroke units in recovery times by a significant amount.

"If you have a look at this slide you can see pre– versus post–functional MRIs of patients engaging and not engaging in the arcade games. What we're looking at is just resting state, or, if you will, the default network structures of these individuals. We're not asking them to engage in any activity while in the scanner, we're simply looking at how their brains are in a resting state both before and after hospitalization therapy, our program"

By this point my head was really hurting and it had begun to spin. I was feeling better but I was certainly not ready to begin a new career in neurology. Dr. White continued to show "brain activation sites," whatever those were, as I slipped out of the auditorium.

As I slowly made my way down the hall, I could not help but appreciate how lucky I was to have been brought to this hospital, and marveled at what a revolutionary program was being undertaken here. But mostly, I longed for an Advil and a soft pillow and maybe some breakfast.

I passed the games room again. I thought I could handle my headache for another minute or two. I wanted to have a quick look around the room, now that I knew its purpose. It was really a bright room and if I were eight again I would have thought I had died and gone to arcade heaven. A room full of free games. Bright lights and activities in each corner of the room, more than I had noticed on my first pass. Between two of the games was a steel door marked Training Lab. I thought, well, if this is going to give me a leg up in getting back to 100% then I'm certainly going to give it my best.

I walked over to Pac-Man, a game I knew well but hadn't played since I was a teenager. I certainly remembered the arcade experience. It was our hangout when I was a kid. I felt kids were so isolated these days. The internet has been called a tool bringing people together, but I think in many cases it has been an isolating factor for individuals who otherwise would have been out of the house and interacting in their community. Many of the kids I saw getting in trouble today seemed isolated and spent a lot of time alone, living in an online world, where there were often no rules.

Anyway, let's give Mr. Pac-Man a try, I thought. I pushed the button and began, using my left hand because my right was still tingling so I thought I should rest it. I did not last long. After a couple of games, I called it quits and headed back down the hall toward my room. How awesome it would have been as a kid to just hit the button and play over and over, no quarters required.

As I got closer, I could see a bit of a commotion in the hall, and I didn't think this much activity was a good sign. That certainly made me realize that I was still in the hospital and I guess things can change at any minute. I thought for the first time that I should give my daughter a call and let her know where I was and what was happening. I also thought my ex-wife would want to know. Though we had parted ways it was never on bad terms; we just grew apart. And maybe also because I was never home. And also because what she wanted and what I needed to do with my life were two different things. She was never well suited to my shift work, the hours I kept. I'm sure she secretly thought I should quit and find a new line of work, especially since we had a little girl to look after, but I liked what I did and I think she should have tried harder. In the middle of this thought, the nurse named Sarah appeared in front of me.

"Detective Myles, you're back!"

"Yes, I am, and thank you for helping me get up and stretch my legs. I really appreciate it."

"No problem. Ah, we have a bit of a situation happening in your room right now."

"I can see that. Is everyone okay?" I asked.

"I'm not sure, but just to limit the number of bodies in the room would you mind just hanging out here for a moment or two?" she said, indicating a lounge on my right, "while they sort things out? There's a recliner in there that's quite comfy, and I'll bring you some water."

"Sure, no problem," I replied. "Could I also have an Advil or aspirin or something? My head is a little sore."

"Certainly." She headed down the hall and disappeared through a doorway.

As I moved to the lounge, I wondered why hospital staff always answered "I'm not sure" to the question "Is everything okay?" when in fact they know things are not okay. I imagine their argument might be, "why do people ask if everything's okay when they can clearly see everything is not okay?" I guess as a detective I was used to getting the facts when I asked a question. However, since I was now a patient, I was not afforded the same status... I was just another zombie in a hospital gown.

I wondered who it was that was in distress in my room. My thought was that it was most likely the heavy-set man in the far corner. That sort of individual often doesn't fare well—I've been at a lot of scenes of medical distress, and the victim is often an overweight male that age. I have also noticed over the years they often die near or in the bathroom; not a great scene, that's for sure.

Sarah returned with water, two tablets, and what looked to be a very comfortable pillow. "Here you go, Detective Myles. If you can just hang out here for a bit I will be back to get you when the room is clear."

"No problem." I hesitated, then added, "Any chance for some breakfast in a little while?"

"Yes, of course. Trays should be up shortly and I'll send yours in here." And with that she was gone. I took the tablets and had a good drink of water, and then placed the pillow behind my head and reclined my chair. Oh, that was nice. If it weren't for being in the hospital with a life-threatening condition, I would have thought I was on holiday. Boy, do I need to take vacation more often. I would have a quick rest and then give Leia a call. I would just have to think of the best way to let her know where her dad was and why. I would most likely tell her I was in the hospital for a procedure for something routine. Or maybe an appendix issue would be a good excuse. The only problem was that that girl was too smart for her own good—she could read me even better than her mother could. Oh, that girl. I had a slightly lopsided smile on my face as I dozed off.

CHAPTER 7

CASEY

Casey Johnson's sister, Cassandra, was in a taxi on the way to Lakefield General Hospital. She had spent the night on a plane to get to Casey by morning. She had limited information about Casey's condition, but it was clear that it was grave. Cassandra had spent much of her traveling time thinking about her little sister, whom she secretly adored for the strength she possessed to go her own way and do her own thing. But now she wished Casey had not gone so far away.

Cassandra had been visibly upset at times during her flight, prompting the woman sitting next to her to gently inquire if she was alright. Cassandra had been silent for several long moments. "My sister's in the hospital. I don't even know what's wrong, but they think it's bad."

"I'm so sorry. I didn't mean to intrude."

Cassandra thought about what she might say about Casey. After several minutes gathering her thoughts, Cassandra continued. "It's alright. Her name's Casey, and she's... the best description I can give of Casey is that she's a beautifully flawed individual with a multitude of complex emotions which can only really be seen by spending long periods of time with her. You certainly couldn't understand her by spending a day or two with her, which is why I think she always kept relationships short. I guess like many of us she lacked the self-awareness to understand how and why she moved from town to town and why men rarely stayed in her life for any duration. Casey is one of those people who believes the cliché that keeping people at a distance and changing towns and men regularly can make you feel safe."

Cassandra's seatmate was awe struck at the in-depth information provided to a complete stranger, but she could not help herself and thus she asked "Safe from what?"

"I guess safe from feeling rejected, safe from being hurt. We never had a great relationship with our parents—they were pretty cold and detached, and nothing we ever did was good enough for them. Casey, I guess, craved the instant gratification that comes from superficial relationships and daily pleasures, because that is all she really knew. Her first few relationships were filled with a lot hurt and that certainly didn't help." Cassandra folder her arms across her chest and turned to the window, and the woman didn't pursue the conversation. Cassandra drifted through thoughts of Casey while staring at the wisps of cloud just below the plane.

Cassandra arrived at the hospital and paid the driver an extra $20 for getting her there quickly. As she stepped through the front doors she was hit by the smell of food, which she found odd because she was expecting that overpowering "hospital smell" of heavy cleaning solutions and bad food standing in steam trays.

But Lakefield General appeared to be a progressive hospital with an almost mall-like appearance, at least on the main floor, including a large food court close to the front entrance offering various well-known fast food restaurants. The entrance area was very large so it took Cassandra a minute to take it all in. But she had no idea where to go. She spotted an older man at a small desk, on which there was a laptop computer and a spiral notebook. On the front of this desk was a yellow and black sign asking, "Have A Question?"

As Cassandra approached the man smiled. His hospital badge identified him as a volunteer. She asked, "I wonder if you can help me. I need to find out where my sister is. All I know is that she was brought in last night."

"Can I have her name, please, Miss?"

Cassandra gave Casey's name and waited nervously as the man typed it in and clicked a couple of times. "Okay, I found her. She's going to be in our new Integrated Stroke Research and Care Center, which is in Wing A on the sixth floor."

"Stroke care? Are you sure?"

The man turned his screen so Cassandra could see. "Yes. This system is updated automatically when patients are moved around and that's currently where she's listed."

"Thank you" Cassandra replied in a daze. She turned and looked helplessly around the busy foyer-mall, which had many hallways and staircases leading in all directions. "How do I get there?"

The volunteer explained, "You are in Wing B currently. There's a bank of elevators over there. Take one of those up to the sixth floor. When you get off turn right, and right again, and go down the hallway toward Wing A. That should take you right to the Stroke Center nursing station. There are signs. And there are people like me near the elevators and various other places," he said reassuringly. "If you get muddled, just ask. That's what we're here for."

"Thank you," she said again, and made her way to the elevators.

As the doors opened on the sixth floor Cassandra immediately saw the signs directing her toward the Integrated Stroke Research and Care Unit. She followed the yellow footprints on the floor that matched the yellow signs. As she walked, she thought Casey could not have had a stroke; it didn't make sense. She was a relatively young woman—there's no way. Maybe they didn't have a bed for her anywhere else, she thought. She hoped.

It was approaching 8:00 AM when Cassandra reached the Stroke Center nursing station. "I'm looking for my sister, Casey Johnson. I was told she's here? I'm her sister," she said redundantly, "Cassandra Resnick."

The woman at the desk wore a badge that said "Caroline B., RPN." She checked the computer. "Yes, she's here. She's in intensive care as she just came out of surgery last night and she needs to be under close observation."

"Surgery? What happened to her? Was there some sort of accident? I have no idea what's going on; they just told me to come. Can someone tell me what's going on?" Cassandra was tired and on the brink of breaking down.

"Dr. Montoya is looking after Casey. I'll page him and let him know you're here. If you can just wait a few minutes, he'll be here shortly and will explain the situation to you."

"Can't you just say what's wrong with her?"

"It's really supposed to come from the doctor. I'm sorry about that."

The nurse offered Cassandra a seat and a cup of coffee. She gratefully accepted the coffee but she could not sit. She paced as she waited nervously for this Dr. Montoya to arrive. The hope that Casey was in this ward by mistake, or because of a lack of space elsewhere, had faded. Cassandra was now struggling with devastating thoughts of Casey being confined to a hospital bed for months on end. If she'd had a stroke, would she be... normal again? Cassandra didn't know how she was going to cope with all this. How was she supposed to care for Casey if she lived on the other side of the country? But there was no one else. What was she going to do? Would she bring her home? She would have to, Casey couldn't go into an institution, but... There were just too many unknowns.

Gerard Montoya was in his office when he received a page indicating that Casey Johnson's family member had arrived. He was just going over Dr. Craig's surgery notes for Casey and he did not like what he saw. Craig had noted that he abandoned the idea of performing an endoscopic evacuation in favor of a craniotomy, noting the patient was young enough to handle the recovery from the surgery and also because he wanted to evacuate the blood from the subarachnoid space quickly to help reduce damage as quickly as possible. Dr. Montoya thought it was probably also true that Craig was more comfortable with the craniotomy and his ability to perform it. A younger surgeon might have opted for the endoscopic evacuation to limit the chance of failure.

Dr. Montoya also read that Dr. Craig had located the rupture and had placed a clip there, but was concerned at the amount of time the patient had been hemorrhaging. As a result, he listed her prognosis as very poor. Craig wrote in his "opinion" note that if she did recover, she would likely have significant impairment. But Dr. Montoya knew that like most surgeons, Craig noted the worst and hope for the best.

Dr. Montoya headed to the sixth floor to talk with the family member. Since the inception of this dedicated unit and because of the specialized equipment and speed of treatment, he was often able to deliver relativity positive news. But one thing you learn quickly as a physician is that you cannot control how the body will react to treatment and all you can do is follow your training and try to get the best outcome by going with the best solutions, usually based on statistics for similar cases.

Dr. Montoya entered the intensive care unit. He glanced at Caroline, who gestured toward Cassandra. When Dr. Montoya saw her, he realized he could have spotted her easily because of how much she looked like the patient.

"I'm Dr. Gerald Montoya. Ms. Johnson is your...?"

"Sister. I'm Cassandra." She extended her hand automatically.

"Okay. So I was on call when Ms. Johnson arrived last night and I've been following her treatment since then. Please be assured that we have moved with great care and speed to help your sister." He directed Cassandra into the lounge. "Please—sit down."

Dr. Montoya turned to Cassandra and explained matter-of-factly. "Casey has had a stroke—a spontaneous intracerebral hemorrhage—which resulted in the rupture of a blood vessel deep inside her brain, in the medial and lateral lenticulostriate arteries."

Cassandra felt her body go weak.

"What this means is that Casey had blood leaking into her brain. It may have been slow at first but a rupture did occur, resulting in a significant amount of blood covering much of the brain's left side. The spaces inside her brain that are normally filled with cerebrospinal fluid filled with blood. Because blood becomes highly toxic to brain cells when it gets outside the blood vessels, it would have killed brain cells within and around this area. That means damage has occurred to the brain."

Cassandra began to cry quietly. Dr. Montoya reached for the box of tissues on a table in the corner and handed it to her.

"In many cases the brain may recover if the bleeding is stopped or controlled quickly. But when there is prolong exposure of blood on the brain itself, and particularly if it' persistent, like with a hemorrhagic stroke, then this bleeding will cause irreversible damage to areas of the brain that are affected." He paused to let Cassandra absorb this news. "This damage—most likely—is significant in your sister's case. We did do surgery on her last night."

Cassandra covered her face with her tissue-stuffed hands and shook her head as if trying to negate everything. She could say nothing.

The doctor continued. "The amount of damage to the brain, well, we won't know for some time because she's in a coma right now. But we are keeping a close watch on her. I also need to let you know that in cases such as Casey's there is a chance that she could also experience some complications, which could include more bleeding. Rates for that are sometimes as high as 30%. The concern of this happening to Casey will be within the next twenty-four to thirty-six hours." He waited again until he was sure she was able to process what he was going to say. "If she starts bleeding again, it's more than likely that it could be fatal."

Cassandra folded her body, pressing her face into her knees. It could not be true. It could not. But she took a deep breath, sat up, and wiped her face. She looked at the doctor, who seemed to have more to say. What more could there possibly be?

"The other concern I have for Casey is a condition called cerebral vasospasm. This is a condition where blood vessels away from the damaged area can become narrow and blood flow becomes blocked, because of all the other things going on in the brain. And so additional areas of the brain would then not be receiving a supply of blood, and this can cause additional damage. This condition can be treated but at the risk of causing rebleeding in other areas because of the types of medication we would use to help open of the area where the blockage occurred.[26] Now this is only a possibility—so far, it hasn't happened yet.

"I can tell you that our most experienced neurosurgeon, Dr. Craig, operated on Casey last night and he was able to clip the area of the bleed and he was able to drain the leaked blood from her brain and reduce complications related to the swelling of the brain. Dr. Craig did note that the bleeding seemed to have been occurring for some time, because of the amount of blood. So her condition must have gone unnoticed for a while."

The thought of Casey suffering alone, with no one to help her, was devastating for Cassandra.

"With strokes, quicker recognition of the condition and getting to the hospital sooner always helps significantly. But as I said, right now it's too soon to tell what the results will be. When she did arrive, she was diagnosed quickly by our on-call physicians. So that's good." Dr. Montoya was a bit uncomfortable with Cassandra's silence. Usually family members have a lot of questions. So he continued. "Dr. Craig would have come and talked to you directly, but he spent several hours in surgery last night with your sister so he headed home an hour ago to get some sleep. When he comes back in, I can have him come speak with you, if you wish."

Cassandra vaguely shook her head and shrugged. She didn't know; it didn't matter.

"I understand that I've just given you an information overload, but I find it best not to hold anything back and to provide as much information as I can up front so families are as up to date as we are on their loved one's care. Do you have any questions?"

Cassandra just looked at Dr. Montoya. She was stuck on the word "fatal." Fatal, she thought. My sister might die. She immediately had feelings of guilt. Just minutes ago she had been worried about the impact of caring for Casey on her own life. Meanwhile, Casey might not have a life at all. Cassandra knew Dr. Montoya was waiting for some type of response, but she didn't know what to say. What was the normal response in a situation like this? "Can I see her?"

"Of course. I'll show you to her room. There are currently three other patients in the room with her, and it is an intensive care ward, so just be aware that the patients all have a number of machine hooked up to them, including your sister, and nurses will be coming and going, so it's all very medical and not really the best place to visit. But I do encourage you to talk to her, even though she's still unconscious, and spend time with her as long as you want."

Dr. Montoya took Cassandra around the corner and through a set of double doors marked Intensive Care. There was another sign on the door indicating no cellphones. The doctor said, "Traditionally most hospitals have restricted these areas, but the philosophy at Lakefield General is to make sure family has access to the patient as much as possible."

Casey was in the first room to the right. Cassandra could see her in the first bed on the left. The morning light coming through the window illuminated the far side of the room. Casey was covered in several hospital blankets and her head was completely bandaged. A few strands of her long, black hair were coming out here and there. Cassandra had the unsettling feeling that much of Casey's head had been shaved to allow for surgery. It made her sad to think of Casey missing so much hair.

Casey appeared to be resting comfortably, but Cassandra couldn't equate what she had just been told with comfort, and she knew it was a coma, not mere sleep. A number of machines stood around the bed, some of which had large screens apparently monitoring Casey's pulse, blood pressure, oxygen levels, and who knew what else. Tubes and wires trailed from the machines and disappeared under the blankets.

Cassandra pulled a chair toward the bed and sat down. She touched Casey's hand. It felt cold, though her hands were never warm. She looked so helpless lying there. She had always been the picture of strength for Cassandra, even though Casey was the younger sister. Cassandra thought how their relationship had always seemed to work the other way around: Casey was often the one to give sound advice to Cassandra.

Cassandra grasped Casey's hand with both of hers and said very softly, leaning toward Casey, "It's me, Cassandra. I'm here and I'm going to take care of you, you just need to get better. I need you, Casey, I cannot think of you not being right there for me. I would be lost without you so you need to fight this and you need to make it out of here." As she whispered, tears began to stream down her face. Everything seemed so surreal. They had talked on the phone just yesterday, and here she was lying in a hospital bed in such a fragile condition. Fatal.

Cassandra continued to speak despite the tears. "Casey, I love you and I will take care of you. I don't care what I need to do, I will get you anything you need. Just please don't go, please please, Casey, don't go." She buried her face in the blankets, sobbing quietly.

As she sat by her sister's side, Cassandra was flooded with thoughts of their childhood, the things they used to do together, the times they spent talking out their problems, so many hours spent talking about the boys, and later the men, in their lives.

Cassandra recalled the day Casey left home. She had been dating a much-older guy for a couple of months. Mostly she saw him on the weekends, but the family didn't see much of him at all. He was always buying her expensive things—watches, jewelry, clothes; basically, anything she liked he would buy for her. They went to the best clubs and sat in VIP areas, and though she was underage that never mattered: when you spent a lot of money at a club it didn't seem to matter how old your date was. She looked old enough and that was what counted.

Cassandra had discovered that Casey's "guy" was married, with two kids. But Casey didn't care. He was nice to her and gave her lots of nice things. However, his trips to their town were going to come to an end because his office there was closing. But he offered her an apartment in his city. The fact that the city was on the other side of the country suited Casey just fine. She was chaffing under the rules at home and wanted to leave, and this was her way out.

He set her up with a job at friend's bar, which led to her deciding to make bartending her career. To Casey, his married status was temporary: he told her many times he was planning to leave his wife; he was just looking for the right time. But there was always some special occasion, and his kids were an issue as well, and he kept putting it off.

Cassandra had told Casey on the phone on many occasions that he was a goddamn liar, but she would not listen. She truly believed he was going to leave his wife for a seventeen-year-old girl in due time; meanwhile, she didn't mind having free nights to party and she always made friends quickly. She took classes to get her bartending license during those days. She loved it from the start. Cassandra recalled the excitement in Casey's voice as she explained about working in a great club, she loved the music, she loved the crowds, she loved the attention she got every night.

But the fairytale came to an end one day when her married man broke things off, including cutting off the money, the gifts, and the rent on her apartment. One day they were just all gone. She never had told Cassandra what exactly happened, but what Cassandra had surmised from their conversations was that his wife had found out about her and gave him an ultimatum, and that rarely works out well for the other girl.

Cassandra had once asked Casey how she could have gotten involved with a married man. Casey's reply was interesting: she told Cassandra that him being married was not her concern, it was his. The fact that he was married did not change what they had, and what they had was special, what she felt was special, and how he made her feel was special. She was not betraying anything sacred because she was not the one who was married. She also believed there was no love in his marriage and she gave him the attention he craved. Casey did not believe she was creating or adding to anyone's problems. She looked after herself and she was good at that.

A nurse touched Cassandra lightly on the shoulder, startling her. "Can I get you anything? Some water?"

Cassandra lifted her head from Casey's bed. "Oh—I guess I dozed off." She pulled out her phone to check the time. Only about forty-five minutes had passed since she came into Casey's room. "Yes, that would be great. Water would be great." She didn't know what to do at this point. She knew she should go eat something but then the thought repulsed her. And she needed to get some real sleep. But she didn't want to leave Casey; she seemed so helpless. Cassandra ached for her sister to sit up and say, "Hey sis, let's get the hell out of here. This place is boring." But she remained motionless. It was too much to bear.

But, Cassandra thought, she needs me here and I'm not going to run away. The nurse returned with a cup of water, which Cassandra drank down with great urgency. She had not realized she was so thirsty. She sat looking at Casey for a while, and realized Casey wasn't going to wake up in the next while. She decided to go to Casey's apartment and maybe take a nap and get something to eat.

She checked Casey's bedside table and found a clear plastic bag containing Casey's belongings. Looking through the bag, she found Casey's work shirt, with her nametag. So she had been at work when it happened. She found Casey's keys, but then decided to take the whole bag. Casey would want some fresh clothes when she woke up. Cassandra had not been to Casey's new place yet, though Casey had been there for a while. That thought made Cassandra think she was a bad sister. She was going to make up for that now.

Cassandra went back down to the lobby. Turning the corner to the food court made her realize she was starving. She found a bank of vending machines and got a bottle of vitamin water and some nuts. She sat down in one of the big comfortable chairs.

As she crunched the nuts she stared out the window and started to work out of plan for getting Casey back home. They could clear out the office area and that could be her room while she healed. Maybe after she got better, she could get a place close by and they could spend more time together. Things would be much better; they could be close again. Cassandra realized her vision for their future was not only about Casey. It was also somewhat selfish. She needed Casey around because she wanted to leave her husband but didn't think she was strong enough to do it on her own. With Casey back home she would have the strength and when Casey was better Cassandra would have her support and help, and their lives would be so much better. She just needed to get her home.

As she finished her snack, Cassandra heard a page for Dr. Montoya to come to the Stroke Center ICU, "code blue." She thought, it can't be Casey. I was just there and she was sleeping peacefully. She got back on the elevator as quickly as she could anyway, and then jogged down the hall to the nursing station.

Caroline, the nurse, said "Please wait here. We're dealing with a situation in your sister's room and we needed room to work."

Caroline picked up a phone but before she could say anything, Cassandra asked in a small voice, "Is it Casey?"

"I am not sure; I haven't been in."

Caroline dashed from the desk to help with the emergency, leaving Cassandra pacing, waiting for her return, waiting for anyone.

Caroline returned briefly. "I've spoken with Dr. Montoya and they are working on Casey. She's in some distress but they are doing what they can. I'm sure Dr. Montoya will speak with you when he has an opportunity. Best thing is to just wait here." She hurried back down the hall, and Cassandra sank into the chair she had occupied when she first arrived.

Chapter 8
Thomas

Ella Batton waited impatiently for the nurse who was supposed to take her to the ward where Thomas was resting. As she waited, she paced around the lounge, still hugging Thomas's quilt. Finally, Ella saw someone in white coming.

"You're Mrs. Batton?" Ella nodded. "I'm Jeffrey. I'm a nurse in the Stroke Research and Care Center. Mr. Batton is settled in the intensive care ward now. Shall we?" He indicated they should walk, and Ella followed him.

"Don't be alarmed that he's in intensive care—mostly he's doing quite well. But it's early yet, so we want him under constant watch for now."

"Thank you," said Ella.

Jeffrey could see Ella's concern, so continued to speak in an effort to ease her worries. "I'm sure Dr. White explained the procedure Thomas underwent. If you've thought of any questions, I will answer if I can. Thomas is still sedated and will be sleeping and resting for the next while but we encourage you to go in and see that he's resting comfortably. All his vital signs are good and he has good oxygen saturation levels, which tells me he keeps in good shape."

They'd reached the Stroke Center. Ella followed Jeffrey to the right and down the hall past the nursing station, and then to Thomas's room. "Your husband is in a ward with another patient right now." Jeffrey let Ella enter the room first, then followed and pulled the privacy curtain around the bed to give Ella some privacy with Thomas.

Ella was relieved to see Thomas despite his hospital accessories—tubes, wires, IV. The first thing Ella did was place the quilt over Thomas to make sure he was cozy, since it was fairly cool in the room. Ella checked Thomas over. He appeared to be in good condition, as far as she could tell. His machines were humming along. She looked at his pulse rate and his blood pressure, for which new measurements appeared at regular intervals. To her, everything looked fine. Nurses came and went, dealing with the other patient, a large man asleep in the bed beside Thomas, and didn't interfere with Ella and Thomas. A woman labeled "Caroline B., RPN" checked Thomas's IV and machines at one point and asked "Can I get you anything?" Ella replied "no thank you" and smiled. As the Nurse left, she added "If you need anything please just ask, and Mam you are permitted to stay as long as you like".

Ella thought staying as long as she liked was quite a good change from the normal hospital routine of years ago. She was pleased that the staff seemed so helpful and made an effort to ensure she was okay. After a while Jeffrey stopped in to see how Ella was doing. She was sitting next to Thomas holding his hand, leaning back in her chair with her eyes closed by this time. Jeffrey touched her ever so lightly on the shoulder, causing Ella to open her eyes instantly. "Mrs. Batton, I know you want to stay close by, and you are more than welcome to hang around here with Thomas, but we also have a lounge just down the corridor here with some comfortable chairs that recline, plus some snacks and drinks, which I am guessing would be something you could use. Maybe you could get a little rest and get some food into you. I can let the other nurses know where you are so we can get you when Thomas comes around."

Ella thought for a moment. She needed to call her daughters and update them and she could not do that here. She also needed to have something to eat, she realized. "That's wonderful. Thank you so much. I could use a bite to eat." She stood and followed Jeffrey. He showed her to the lounge.

"So, I'm going off shift now," he said, "but I will see you again in the morning."

Ella looked at the vending machines in the lounge. Their offerings included a number of microwavable noodle meals. She chose the one that sounded like it might be the least spicy. She found it ironic that such a high-sodium prepackaged meal would be offered in the stroke wing. She got a drink and sat down with her food. She pulled out her phone to start making her calls, but the thought of talking to anyone was exhausting.

Ella took a few bites of noodles and a sip of her juice and was about to call her eldest daughter, when Susan appeared in the doorway. "Susie! You're here! That's lovely. But I told you not to bother!"

Susan answered softly, "I told you I would come. I've actually been here awhile but I waited because the nurse said both of you were resting. That sounded like a good thing so I waited."

Ella gave Susan a big hug. She felt she might start crying, but held her breath to keep it at bay. She didn't want Susan to worry.

Ella sat with Susan and tried to explain what Dr. White had told her about her dad's recovery, focusing mainly on the positive details, such as the likelihood that he would regain normal functioning and that they had arrived at the hospital quickly, which was a good thing. Ella could not remember all the medical details but did her best to explain what she had heard. She was so relieved that Susan was there and that she had someone to talk to.

They sat together for some time before Susan had to go. "I'll be staying here tonight," Ella said. "The nurses will let me know if anything changes, and I'll call you. When you go home, I want you to call your sisters."

"I will. But I want to go in and see Dad for a bit before I go." Ella got up to accompany her. "No, you stay here and finish that amazing lunch." She winked at her mother. "I'll be back tomorrow right after I get the kids off to school."

After Susan left, Ella finished her food and settled into one of the large recliners. She quickly fell fast asleep. Not long after, Caroline came by with a warm blanket and covered her up.

***

Bright and early morning light flashed through the windows sporadically as clouds sailed past the sun. Thomas slowly opened his eyes. He noticed the wires and tubes attached to him, but realized he was comfortable despite them. He knew Ella must be close by when he saw the quilt. Ever so slightly, Thomas flexed each hand. His right hand readily flexed with good strength, but the left seemed somewhat weak. But he was able to move it, which he thought was remarkable. He remembered it being quite numb yesterday. Thomas struggled to sit more upright. He was unsure of whether it was a struggle because he had been lying still for so long or because of his condition.

As he sat up a bit more, he could see he was not alone—there were now three other patients in the room. On the other side of the room was a woman who appeared to be in a deep sleep, lying flat. The patient directly across from him was a man. To Thomas's left the curtain was partially drawn so Thomas was unable to see that patient, except for foot-shaped lumps in the bed.

Thomas knew it must be fairly early—he was sure he was seeing dawn light. He saw a cup on his bedside table, reached for it, and took a sip. Thomas guessed that Ella must be asleep in a chair somewhere. He wished she had gone home to get a proper rest, but knew she wouldn't have. He thought, maybe I'll just lie here and rest a little longer and then see if I can find out where she is. Thomas lay back down, his mind busy wondering about so many things, then resting and dozing.

He woke to the sound of people in the room: nurses and doctors were gathered around the bed beside him. The curtain had been drawn but he could hear the urgency and concern in their voices. Another nurse arrived with another piece of equipment. Eventually the commotion died down and the staff left.

Thomas maneuvered himself up to a sitting position. He wondered if he would be allowed to get up. He pushed his call button. A nurse came in quickly. "Wow! That was fast."

"Good morning, Mr. Batton. I'm Mazie, a nurse here in the Stroke Center. How are you feeling?"

"Pretty good, actually." As he spoke, Thomas felt a little weakness on the left side of his face, as well as in his arm and hand, and he thought his speech might be a little sloppy. He was sure it felt odder than it appeared, like when you come back from the dentist with your face frozen and you're convinced it looks grotesque but when you look in the mirror you see it's surprisingly normal. "Do you know if my wife is around here somewhere?"

"Indeed she is. She's just down the corridor in the lounge having a rest."

Thomas nodded as if he knew that was exactly what she was going to say. He touched the left side of his face. "Say, does my face look... weird? Because it feels... not quite right."

"Don't worry, that feeling will pass. You look fine. And you're doing well."

"If you say so..."

"Since you've had a stroke on the right side of your brain it's normal to have weakness in various areas on the left side of your body."

"Yes, my left hand is... a little off, but otherwise I'm feeling... not bad."

"Good! I can help you get steady on your feet if you want, and then you can go down to the lounge and wake up Mrs. Batton." Thomas thought this was a splendid idea, though he was apprehensive about Ella noticing the difference on the left side of his face.

Mazie removed a couple of wires connecting him to monitors and checked his IV. "Okay, all set. Are you ready to get up and get moving?"

"Yes, thank you. I can't miss my daily walk, now can I?" Mazie helped Thomas up, and helped him navigate his way to the door.

Once they were in the hallway, Mazie said, "Dr. White is here this morning. She's tied up right now but will be on the ward later to chat with you and Mrs. Batton."

"Thank you."

After they had taken several slow steps, Mazie ensured that Thomas was steady on his feet and then directed him to the lounge where Ella was resting. "Do you want me to stick with you till you get there, or are you comfortable on your own?"

"I think my legs are working okay. I don't think I'll have any trouble. It's not far."

"Excellent. But just holler if you need help." And with that she returned to the nursing station.

Thomas sort of shuffled cautiously to the lounge, and inside was Ella, covered with a flannel hospital blanket and reclined in a big chair. As on most mornings when he found her like this at home, he enjoyed watching her have a good sleep. Thomas made his way over to her and sat on the arm of the chair next to hers. He put his hand on her leg, leaned in, and gave Ella a big kiss on the cheek, just as he did every morning.

"Ella, are you going to sleep all morning or are we going for a walk?"

Ella briefly thought she was at home and Thomas had caught her sleeping on the couch again. But as she opened her eyes she immediately remembered where she was—and why. She was surprised to see Thomas hovering over her, but greatly relieved. In a sudden flood of emotion, Ella didn't know how to respond beyond welling up with tears and reaching up to give Thomas a big hug and a kiss. Finally she said, "Thomas. What are you doing out of bed? Do you know you had a stroke?"

REALLY? I HAD A STROKE?

Thomas laughed. "Good morning to you too, Ella. Yes, I know what happened. I was reminded this morning and I recall I was also told several times yesterday. But I was also told this is the best place to be if you've had a stroke. Good thing we don't live in the middle of nowhere or you might be short one husband today."

"This is no time to joke," said Ella, pulling her chair upright. "How are you feeling?"

"Not too bad, actually. My left hand and arm seem a little weak, my mouth on the left feels a little off, and I'm sure it looks a little off—I notice it as I speak. Did they tell you all that happened?"

"Yes they did, but I don't think I remember everything the doctor said. They mentioned you had a blockage on the right side of your brain, I think in a couple of places, but they were able to use some special medication and that helped clear the blockages and get the blood flowing again. She said you had the good kind of stroke. Or at least, the less-bad kind."

"Ah, okay. Well obviously they did a good job because I'm up already and moving remarkably well, I'd say," Thomas replied happily.

Ella smiled. "Yes, it's amazing. Dr. White said you were healthy otherwise, which helped a lot. She also said we have an option to get some therapy and get you back to a hundred percent."

"A hundred percent? Hmm. Not sure I want to be better than I was before, that might throw off our balance!"

Ella was feeling more relieved with each moment. "I can see your humor has not been effected." Tears returned to her eyes. "Oh Thomas. I'm so glad you're okay. I was so scared. I kept thinking you'd end up like my cousin, after his stroke. Such a tragedy." He squeezed her hand. "Susan was here last night; she went in to see you while you were asleep. She said she would be back this morning after she got the kids to school."

"Oh, you shouldn't have bothered Susan. I'd rather have a day or two before the kids see. I mean, I'm up, but my face is weird and I think my speech... I'd just prefer they not have to see this."

Ella did in fact notice a small issue with his speech. "Thomas, you had a stroke. I had to call the kids and let them know—at least so they knew where we were. They know what happened, so they won't be surprised. They probably think it's worse than it is! Plus, I needed to talk to someone and I was scared..."

"Okay, of course I understand. I'm sorry. It was pretty scary. I'm not really sure how to handle all this right now, and I'm just happy to be up and about and I wish we could just get back home and get back to normal. But I know things won't be normal for a while. I just don't want everyone worrying."

Ella reassured him. "I know, Thomas, I know. Don't worry. We will figure it all out just like we have figured everything else out. The nurse told me Dr. White was busy this morning but she would be by later to talk to us and let us know how you're doing. Apparently, as I've heard from the other staff, she is very good, like, one of the best in the country, so I think we're lucky and we're in good hands. She—the doctor—said yesterday that this hospital has a number of rehabilitation programs, so we can get you signed up to help you get everything back to normal. I knew you would be interested in it simply because you are interested in everything. You can treat this as your new hobby."

Thomas shifted off the arm of the chair and sat down properly, reclining his chair a bit. He let out a big sigh. "Well, that sounds like a great idea, Ella. I love a good challenge." He was making an effort to sound brave, but part of him was concerned that he would not regain all his energy, let alone his functions, and he wondered how this was all going to affect him in the end. He watched Ella assessing the coffee possibilities offered by the lounge's machines. After a minute or two of silence he said, "Ella?"

"Mm?"

"What do you say we go for our morning coffee?"

"Really?"

Thomas pushed himself forward to the edge of the chair. "Yes really. I think you need the exercise," he said slyly. "So how about we grab a wheelchair and you can give me a push to the nearest coffee place. If we take a wheelchair, I'm sure the nurses won't give us too much trouble about leaving the floor." Thomas actually didn't think he was quite up to an extended walk so soon, but he thought this might be a good way to get Ella feeling a bit better about being in a hospital at all.

Ella brightened. "Yes, I think that's a great idea. I'll go find a wheelchair and let the nurses know where we are off too. I hope they won't mind. Let me just text Susie and let her know you are up and doing well, and maybe she can meet us for coffee. She will be so happy." She got out her phone and Thomas watched her painstakingly composing her message with one finger.

As Ella left the room Thomas sat back and relaxed. He truly felt lucky that he was doing so well one day after something as potentially devastating as a stroke. He thought of Ella's cousin, unable to speak or move very much, and they knew people who had died of strokes. Maybe it wasn't really luck, but more a matter of the pieces falling together. Apparently he had been brought to the best possible place. Ella had said he had the "good" type of stroke. He had arrived at the hospital quickly. And maybe he was also reaping the benefits of staying in reasonable physical shape.

Ella returned moments later with the wheelchair and helped Thomas into it. "The nurse said there's a nice coffee shop downstairs in the lobby, today we will let you out in the wheelchair but we would like you up and walking soon". Thomas replied "no problem". Ella was pleased that the ward Nurses were quite happy that we're going to be out and about. And stated to Thomas "I can't get over how relaxed they seem to be to let you wander around".

At that moment, a nurse came in and attached Thomas's IV to the stand on the wheelchair. "The breakfast trays should be coming soon, so we'll just hold it for you." And with that they were off.

***

It was almost mid-morning when Thomas and Ella returned to his room. They were waiting for Dr. White. Their trip to the coffee shop had made it feel almost like any other morning, almost. Susan had joined them there and was thrilled to see her dad up and about and in fairly good condition considering he had had a stroke just a day earlier. She promised to update her sisters and let them know everything was going well and there was no urgent need for them to travel to the city at this point.

Thomas had only water, partly to reassure Ella he would stay hydrated and partly because he was unsure of what he could or could not have to eat. Aren't there always restrictions? He figured water was a sure bet. They spent time chatting and people watching, especially what appeared to be a very nervous doctor who looked like he wanted to chat with the barista, but she seemed engrossed in her work, so the exchange was brief and quite awkward. Thomas was rooting for the young doctor and lamented this missed opportunity on his behalf. The lady was cute!

Thomas was relieved to get back to his room and lie down—the excursion has left him tired. A nurse brought in his breakfast and he ate slowly, one-handed, while they waited for Dr. White.

The doctor arrived before too long and entered the room with swift, efficient steps, something that surely came with working at a hospital for so many years. "Mr. and Mrs. Batton, hello." She pulled a chair close to where Ella was sitting at Thomas's bedside. She gave Thomas a pat on his arm as she spoke. "I'm Evelyn White. I'm a clinical neurologist and I saw you when you came in yesterday; you probably don't remember. I'm glad to see you are up and looking much better than yesterday. The nurses tell me you were up and about this morning and even went down for coffee. It's nice to know you felt like being up; that's a good sign. I can tell you many years ago we did not have such good results, even with your type of stroke."

Dr. White then explained in great detail to Thomas what she had told Ella a day earlier about the location of his blockages and the challenges they had treating them. Thomas listened carefully; he planned to do some research on this later and was trying to focus on the details.

"The first forty-eight hours after the stroke are very telling in regards to recovering," Dr. White explained, "and we need to keep a close eye on you for complications that you could experience after receiving thrombolytic medications like the one we gave you, and of course just normal things that might come up after you've had a stroke. I can see you're feeling better, and I'm guessing you do not want to stay here any longer than you have to, but don't be in a rush to leave. I'm planning to keep you another day at least to ensure there are no complications. Plus, I want to take a further scan today and have a look, and we'll follow up with another one tomorrow, and if all looks well, you should be able to go home end of day tomorrow or day after."

"That's wonderful," Ella said.

"You'll have some follow-up appointments, of course," Dr. White continued, "and I'm going to have our research coordinator stop in today and review some of our ongoing projects, which, I understand from your wife, you may be interested in participating in. I certainly recommend that you take advantage of them, because they will allow you access to additional scans, follow-up measurements, and of course, great rehabilitation resources."

Dr. White was very direct and really focused her attention when she met with a patient, giving them the feeling that she genuinely cared and her extensive experience was being used at the upmost to help them. This approach endeared her to patients and provided a level of comfort not often found in anyone, let alone a busy physician. "Now tell me how you're feeling right now, everything you can think of," she said to Thomas.

Thomas described his current condition to Dr. White in detail. "I guess the thing I'm most concerned about is getting my speech back to normal, and the strength in my left arm."

"There are a lot of variables involved in recovering from a stroke. But recent research on getting going quickly with a rehab program points to their effectiveness in assisting with full recovery. That's why I'm having the coordinator stop by today to get you started as soon as possible.

"Our program is really revolutionary, and our success rate in increasing functional ability in patients who make it through the early stages of their stroke is excellent. And you are a prime candidate for the recovery program."

"Really?" Thomas asked, intrigued.

"Yes. Many stroke wards, where they exist at all, offer access to occupational and speech therapists *when possible.* And if they do have access, it is usually for about an hour every other day. This means that many patients spend twenty-three hours of the day in their rooms, isolated, especially if they have no family around, and that means limited success for recovery. For example, you can imagine that a small rural hospital would not have the same access to therapists as a big urban facility.

"At Lakefield General we've been striving to create access for patients and physicians to best-practice research. The new research is telling us that we need to get the brain going and challenged as soon as we can. Most hospitals have a goal of getting patients ambulatory; in other words, if they can feed themselves and get to the washroom, then they can discharge them and get them out the door. Sadly, this is partly based on the fact that the hospital needs the bed for another patient. But my belief is that we need to directly treat the organ that has been injured: the brain. Most hospitals and rehab centers don't train the injured brain because they don't have the expertise and they just keep following the old model of care."

"So we are really lucky we're here, as opposed to another hospital," said Ella.

"For sure," Dr. White agreed. "A lot of the research endorsed here involves activities that are cognitively challenging and activate the brain as much as possible as soon as possible after a stroke. We need to get the brain active and keep it active. Physical activity is crucial too. For example, even when walking is still a concern, we get people up. We've developed equipment where patients can be supported with a harness to help with gait and balance recovery. Exercise is an essential part of any recovery so we definitely encourage safe movement and activities to keep you going, as you saw this morning when the nurses were happy to let you go for coffee."

"Yes, that was lovely," said Thomas, "even though I only had water because I didn't know if coffee was okay."

"It's fine, just don't overdo it. Have you seen our games room?" the doctor asked. It's designed especially for our stroke patients, though if you go at 2:00 AM you might find a few of my research fellows in there once in a while. Anyway, the games room has a number of different activities, but the most obvious are our arcade games. One of our researchers has shown really good success in patients' recovery when they engage in these types of activities, especially when combined with our other initiatives."

"You mean like pinball?" asked Thomas enthusiastically.

"Exactly, and more besides."

"I was pretty good back in the day. Maybe not a wizard, but I had some high scores." He reached out as if holding the corners of a pinball table, squeezing the buttons. His face showed dismay when his left fingers would not cooperate as he liked.

"That's exactly what it's designed to help you with," Dr. White said. "I'm glad you're interested. You can head to the games room anytime—it's just down the hall. I'll have the duty nurse book your scan for later today and I or one of the other neurologists will be back for a chat with you after that about how things look. So do either of you have any questions?" she asked quickly as she got up to leave, giving the impression that she needed to go and hopefully questions could be held till later.

"Not right now," Thomas responded, "but if I have any, I will bring them up later."

"Very well." Dr. White walked briskly from the room.

Thomas and Ella looked at each other after she had left, both clearly reeling from receiving that much information in such a short time. Ella spoke first. "Did you get all that?"

"I think so..."

"She's really quite remarkable."

"So do you think we should go check out this games room?"

Ella shrugged. "I think if you're up to it, we could go and see what's there."

"Well, maybe later. I am very curious about what they want to have us doing. We should go look. Pinball I can handle, but let's see what else is there. Arcade games.

Who knows? Maybe the girls could show me how to play some of those. It will take them back to their childhood," Thomas said with a chuckle. "But right now, I'm actually beat. I think maybe I should take a bit of a nap."

"Me too." Ella slouched down in her chair, leaned back and closed her eyes.

She woke with a start some time later, surprised that she had actually fallen asleep. She took the cup from Thomas's bedside table and went to refill it and find a drink for herself. The sound of her returning woke Thomas from his nap. "Do you think you could help me..." he gestured toward the washroom. Ella helped him to his feet and held his elbow as they crossed the room.

When he was settled back in bed, he asked, "What time is it?"

She pulled her phone from her purse. "12:15. Are you hungry? Maybe we could go back down to that lobby. It looked like they had lots of places to eat. What a change from the old-fashioned hospital cafeteria!"

"I'll say. I wouldn't mind a bit to eat. Maybe we could go have lunch and then check out this games room."

Ella pushed the wheelchair close to the bed. "Shall we?"

Thomas replied "bring it along I will use it if I get tried"

CHAPTER 9
BRUCE

Twenty-four hours after his stroke, Bruce Grafton remained comatose and under close observation after undergoing tPA therapy. The goal was to recanalize a number of significant brain areas by removing blockages. But Bruce's condition was grave; in another hospital a patient like Bruce may already have succumbed to his stroke.

Eli Pattern, the attending neurologist, had authorized the use of intravenous thrombolysis without knowing quite when Bruce's stroke had happened, but Dr. Pattern was aware of recent research suggesting that tPA could be used as long as eight hours after the stroke. And in Mr. Grafton's case, there wasn't much to lose.

Dr. Pattern was heading to the intensive care unit to check on Bruce. He believed that surgery was most likely not an option at this point; they were at the wait-and-see stage. As well, he knew that the surgeon he would have wanted, Fenton (Dr. Craig), had already spent the night in surgery with another patient and so wouldn't want to go back in right away if not really required.

Dr. Pattern was, like many specialists at Lakefield General, an MD/PhD and he believed in using the latest and best research information to maximize clinical effectiveness in his patients. But his research background also meant he knew that no patient reacts exactly the same way as another and that after a stroke, physical variables can fluctuate significantly from one patient to the next. What he had gleaned from current research and his own medical opinion was that being at the end of the blood pressure spectrum often contributed to poor outcomes for the patient. Bruce Grafton's blood pressure was very high.

He also expected a slight increase in body temperature as a result of Bruce experiencing such a significant stroke; what was important was to determine whether the temperature change was strictly stroke related or whether an infection may be a contributing factor. Either way, he knew that a higher post-stroke temperature was related to higher death rates, especially if the individual had been treated with thrombolytic medications, as this patient had.

Interns often asked Dr. Pattern why they didn't use fever-reducing drugs to control a patient's temperature. He would explain that antipyretics could help with a fever but can cause complications related to recovery. Simply keeping the room cool, in addition to applying cooling agents, had been the most effective approach.

Dr. Pattern also wanted to check the patient's latest blood sugar level, which could provide insight into the extent of injury and the brain regions involved. Because the insular cortex region of the brain helps to regulate the neuroendocrine stress response, they could expect to see hyperglycemia if this region had been damaged. Pattern was hoping for the best, but hyperglycemia was associated with a poor prognosis, and he did expect to see it in Bruce Grafton. If Bruce's blood sugar was high, in combination with the severity of his stroke, the use of thrombolytics made it likely that an intracerebral hemorrhage could occur. Pattern knew of the risk, but this patient really had no other options.

Another concern was Bruce's size and whether he may experience significant oxygen shortages at any point. They had left the patient's oxygen on a constant flow to help avoid low oxygen, but during scans or bed transfers this was difficult to control, and Bruce would need another scan today.[27] On the positive side, because this patient was in a dedicated stroke unit, these types of changes were monitored constantly.

Dr. Pattern's main concern was the possibility of an intracerebral hemorrhage, which would certainly be devastating for Bruce. Pattern knew that Bruce would most likely not survive surgery and would not be a good candidate for endovascular coil treatment. His other concern was something he hoped the police had handled overnight, and that was locating next of kin. When the patient was scanned later today, Dr. Pattern wanted to have someone to discuss his condition with. Until the next of kin had been located, Bruce's care was the sole responsibility of Dr. Pattern.

On reviewing the patient's chart and his numbers, which did not look great, and looking at the patient himself, Dr. Pattern believed there had been no real change. He proceeded to his office to call the police district responsible for locating the patient's next of kin. He was transferred from the front desk to the criminal investigation's unit and after another minute or two waiting, a detective picked up his call.

"We put a call in to his employer last night; a trucking company," the detective said. "A dispatcher said nobody with access to human resource files would be in until nine today. So there's a message waiting for them. The dispatcher did say Grafton had an ex-wife, but didn't know anything more, couldn't remember her name, couldn't think of the guy ever mentioning any other family. So basically right now we got nothing. We'll let you know when we do."

Dr. Pattern sighed on hearing this news, but asked the detective to give the desk at the Stroke Center a call as soon as they had some information so he could be paged. He gave the detective a very brief overview of Bruce's condition to impress upon her the urgent need for Dr. Pattern to speak with a next of kin.

***

Later that afternoon Bruce, still unconscious, was loaded onto a gurney headed for the imaging suite just down the hall and around the corner. The location of the imaging suite was unusual; often, imaging equipment, such as a CT and MRI machines, was in first-floor or basement areas of the hospital simply because of their sheer size, in addition to the wiring required. Hospitals also needed this equipment to be easily accessible for emergency patients, which take up the bulk of the scanning time.

But the Stroke Center at Lakefield General had access to the Neurology and Brain Sciences Department imaging suite. Because the majority of research scans were conducted after hours, stroke patients could easily be scheduled when needed and didn't have to be transported far. They did, however, frequently encounter malnourished-looking graduate students, often wearing flip flops and retro concert T-shirts muttering to themselves as they tried to work out the intricacies of their latest experiments.

The primary use of computed tomography is to see where blood and bone are in the body. At its most basic, CT imaging is often ordered by emergency physicians to see if blood and bones are where they're supposed to be. The problem with CTs is that they do not have great resolution, so there are limitations in terms of seeing structural abnormalities, especially if you want to see specific structures in the brain.

Magnetic resonance imaging is costlier and more time consuming and requires a skilled operator. In addition, MRIs require the patient to remain immobile; controlling head movement is essential. MRIs are basically big magnets that work by disrupting the water molecules in the body's structures. After the disruption occurs the water molecules begin to move back to where they are supposed to be and this is when an image is captured. The excellent resolution makes MRI the gold standard for imaging the structures of the brain. But because of the cost, MRI is reserved in many hospitals for specific or dire cases. As a result, CTs are performed even when physicians know an MRI would be a better alternative.

MRI provides stroke neurologists with fine structural detail to help determine the extent of damage. It also provides insight into whether there was existing damage in the brain. If problems such as dementia like or additional stroke-type events develop, the neurologist will have a starting point to determine relative changes.

The staff attending to Bruce Grafton transferred him very careful from the gurney to the MRI table to ensure he did not become hypoxic. Because Bruce was unconscious the technicians operating the MRI would have no concern about problems with the imaging caused by head movement during the scan. Even though Bruce was unconscious, the staff covered him with a blanket—the room was always kept very cool because it was better for the equipment. They carefully inserted a pair of ear plugs as well because the MRI machine makes loud hammering sounds as the magnet turns on and off.

Dr. Pattern wanted to conduct a special "diffusion-weighted" MRI close to the thirty-six hour mark after the stroke, which when combined with Bruce's Stroke Scale score would provide a better understanding of what Bruce's recovery might look like. Dr. Pattern expected the MRI to give him a better idea of the effects of the stroke so he could understand possible changes in the brain and identify major areas affected. He was also looking for recovery and renewed blood flow in previously obstructed areas.

Pattern was also concerned about the extent of the tissue damage, which often occurs around areas of the brain where blood flow has been cut off. He was still concerned about further bleeding. He knew there was evidence that patients with poor initial Stroke Scale scores, delayed treatment time, and high blood pressure, like this patient, were at high risk of bleeding after tPA treatment. But there wasn't much else they could try at this point.

Dr. Pattern decided to retreat to his office to catch up on his notes, and he had a number of dictations that were well overdue. He wanted to get to this work before Bruce's MRI results were completed. Eli thought it might be nice to slip into the on-call room and grab a quick nap, but he had just started his shift so that was really not an option, even though he was tried from being on call last night, and he was on call again tonight. It never fails: when you're most tired the likelihood of getting paged always seems greater. So as a compromise for not getting a nap, he would stop and grab a coffee and a snack at the lobby coffee shop.

Caffeine wasn't the only reason he wanted to stop by the coffee shop. There was a particular new barista he had noticed a few times. He was not sure how old she was but he thought she was around his age; older than the kids who worked there weekends, anyway. She had the most beautiful green eyes and short black hair that had a fresh wavy look to it, like she just got out of the shower. He wasn't sure how she did that but he was keen to find out. Most days she wore form-fitting yoga pants and odd-colored lipstick (like pale blue). And she had the most incredible smile, oh her smile... it was intoxicating.

As Eli waited in line for her to take his order, he daydreamed about having dinner with her, somewhere with soft music with profound lyrics suggesting that this was it: they were meant for each other. There was only one problem, he thought as he got closer to the counter, and that was that eventually he would have to actually talk to her for more than five seconds to ask her out. He was struggling with finding the most tactful way to ask her. I wonder how she smells? he suddenly thought. In a coffee shop it was impossible to tell, because it always smelled like coffee. Maybe she just always smelled like coffee.

He was nervous now. For two weeks he had not known what to say to her. Every conversation he started seemed to focus on the weather. How pathetic was that? He was convinced that this time he would come up with something more interesting, flirtatious even—some conversation that would let her know he was interested. Maybe he could find out a little about her, like if she was interested, or even single. But how? What was the best way to do this? He had never been any good at this. Then he thought, this is ridiculous. I spend all day every day dealing with complex problems, making life or death decisions; this can't be that hard. Can it?

Finally, it was his turn. "Ah, hi, Hi! I'll have a large Colombian with a vanilla shot." He remembered to smile. "Some weather the past few days", oh I thought to myself oh no the weather again.

She said, "Yes, it has been unpleasant recently. Anything else I can get for you today, doctor?"

Eli was frozen for a moment. This is it—just casually say, how about your number? "No, ah, that's all the coffee I need today." After which he thought, what does that even mean? That's all the coffee I need today. She's going to think I'm a patient, not a doctor. What is the matter with me? I can't even ask a girl out. No wonder I'm still single. Now when people ask, "why are you still single," I can reference this brilliant conversation.

The coffee shop was busy as usual and he didn't get a chance to say anything else. His order was on the counter and Miss Barista was on to the next customer, and everyone continued with their day. So he had no choice but to move on, thus he hung his head slightly and walk away.

As Eli walked back to his office, he thought of Oscar Wilde's comment from "The Happy Prince": "I am so clever that sometimes I don't understand a single word of what I am saying." He had even forgotten to order a snack. Way to go genius, he thought. Fortunately, he kept a supply of black licorice in his desk, which would have to do until he could get some lunch. Making do with the candy would also serve as penance for his inability to talk like a human. He sipped his coffee and started on his chart dictations, pleased to be able to get through a number of them, because in a hospital like this it generally wasn't long before you were wanted somewhere.

The phone rang. It was the imaging suite in the Stroke Center, which Eli knew was not a good sign. Lakefield General had an electronic medical record system, enabling several units to review results simultaneously. That provided quicker access for everyone and increased efficiency in patient care. The radiologist said they had just uploaded Bruce Grafton's images and requested that Dr. Pattern have a look right away.

He called up the images from Grafton's medical record. Intracerebral hemorrhage had been his main concern, and that's exactly what he saw on the MRI images.

Dr. Pattern knew he would need to treat Bruce with a medication to encourage coagulation to stop the bleeding. He ordered fresh frozen plasma and was contemplating the use of vitamin K_1 but was unsure of the best course of action because there was limited best-practice evidence for this treatment showing success. Dr. Pattern also knew that with Bruce's risk factors he was looking at a limited chance of recovery anyway. The reality was that Bruce Grafton most likely did not have long. That likelihood raised the doctor's other concern: finding the next of kin. No specific do not resuscitate order was in place for this patient, though he believed that would be the best course of action because any type of recovery was going to mean significant disability and very poor quality of life.

An hour later Dr. Pattern got the call he was waiting for from the police: a Detective Langdon explained that they had found a next of kin for Bruce. "He's got an ex-wife, name of Debbie Imahori. We let her know he was hospitalized with a stroke, so you should be getting a call from her shortly. Also, they had one child, a daughter, age eighteen, who lives with the ex-wife. So she's actually the next of kin and will need to be informed directly, in case of an adverse event. Here's their number." The detective gave Dr. Pattern their phone number and address.

"Thanks, Detective." After Dr. Pattern hung up, he called the nursing station at the Stroke Center to let them know he was expecting a call from Debbie Imahori about Mr. Grafton. As he was speaking, the nurse interrupted.

"Hold on—I see her on call display right now. Hang up and I'll transfer her to you." Dr. Pattern had only a few seconds to compose himself. He was used to delivering bad news to families, but he preferred to have a few moments to compose what he was going to say because delivering the news the right way was important. You had to be succinct but ensure all the information was included, and you had to explain it at a level the individual could understand even while under great stress.

Dr. Pattern picked up the phone. "Dr. Pattern speaking."

"Hello... this is Debbie Imahori. I'm the ex-wife of Bruce Grafton. I understand from the police that he's in the hospital? I guess he still has me listed as his next of kin, but I have to say, we have not spoken in quite some time."

"I'm sorry to hear that, but I have a situation here with Mr. Grafton and I was hoping to explain it to you, or perhaps another family member, so that you could assist with a decision on his care."

Debbie interrupted. "I'm not sure it's my place to make any decisions for Bruce. As I said, we're divorced and have not been in touch for quite some time..."

148

As she spoke Dr. Pattern became concerned, because one thing he did not want at this point was a next of kin who was indecisive. That would not resolve the situation. "Ms. Imahori, please let me explain first. I understand your relationship has ended and so this is complicated, but I want you to know that Bruce's condition is very serious. He has experienced a significant stroke. There was a blockage of blood flow to his brain, and without blood flow the brain is not getting oxygen, resulting in damage. To treat this, we gave him some medication to start the blood flowing again, but the complication was that he seems to have had the stroke some time before help got to him. We don't know exactly how long he had been in his truck before he was taken to the hospital, but it was a while."

"That damn truck, very fitting."

Dr. Pattern continued. "We think what happened is that a piece of arterial plaque, probably from the carotid artery in the neck, broke off and traveled into his brain. The arteries in the brain are much smaller than in the carotid region and so a large piece of plaque can create a serious blockage. In Bruce's case the blockage was in the internal carotid artery, which feeds many regions of the brain. A blockage may result in significant damage to the brain.

"After treating this blockage with medication to restore blood flow, there was bleeding in another part of Bruce's brain. This can happen with this type of treatment, but it resulted in more damage to the brain, because blood outside of the arteries in the brain becomes toxic to cells in the brain. We have started another course of treatment, but I have to say his prognosis is very poor and the damage to his brain is most likely quite significant. If he survives, it is highly likely that he would need around-the-clock care. He will not return to life as he knew it."

Debbie was in disbelief, trying to get a handle on what the doctor was saying. She asked the first question that came to her mind. "Will he be able to return to driving again?" She knew the answer even as she spoke.

"Ms. Imahori, I am not sure how to impress this upon you, but it's likely he will never walk, talk, or even feed himself again."

There was a brief silence, and then Debbie calmly said, "Oh. Okay, I understand. What is it you need from me? I'm not sure what I can do."

"I was hoping to put in place a DNR order—a do not resuscitate order—for Bruce, which means that if he experiences trouble, we would not resuscitate him, and we would let him go. We need a family member to authorize that."

Debbie replied with disbelief, "Oh God! Really? He's going to die? What do I tell my daughter? She's going to be heartbroken. I mean, he didn't see her much sometimes but he has always been there for her. This is going to break her heart. He's her dad! Oh God; what do I tell her?"

"Ms. Imahori, I understand how difficult it is, but my goal, and I hope a goal for you and your daughter, is to think of Bruce. I am hoping that you or your daughter—the police told me she is of age—would authorize the DNR order, which will let us let him go. We believe this is the best course of action here."

Debbie answered quickly. "Dr. Pattern, though Bruce is not my husband anymore this is a very big decision for me to make. I will have to tell Michelle—that's my daughter, his daughter—and we'll have to talk about it.

Leave it to Bruce to screw me over again in his crisis. Why on earth did he leave me as his next of kin? God damn him for that, God damn him... Oh, I'm sorry, I didn't mean that, I'm just kind of in shock. I'm more upset that he also left me to tell his daughter, like he always has. Bruce just..." There was silence on the phone for a while but Dr. Pattern knew it was important not to say anything. He was experienced enough to know that Debbie was running through things in her head.

She said, "He will not drive again," as if confirming.

"It is unlikely that he will walk again, never mind drive."

Debbie took a deep breath and then said, "Let him go. It is what he would want. Just let him go."

Dr. Pattern explained very calmly, "Thank you. I will have my office courier you some paperwork for your daughter to sign, unless you can come in right now, and if you can send it back right away that would be most helpful. And of course, if you or his daughter wish to come and see him, you are welcome anytime."

"Thank you. I believe Michelle will want to come as soon as possible, and I will let her know straight away."

They concluded their conversation and Dr. Pattern prepared the DNR order. The Stroke Center received the signed order an hour and a half later. Dr. Pattern assumed that Bruce most likely would not last much longer but they continued to treat him. Dr. Pattern was hoping that the patient's daughter would get there in time to see him, but he knew, too, that she was going to see her father in the most vulnerable position she had ever seen him in. That's never a good ending, but closure can be very important.

Chapter 10

Declan

I felt warmth on my face and thought it must be the sun coming in the large lounge windows. I stayed in my comfy recliner soaking up the sunlight for a while before I was willing to open my eyes. The light flooding the room was comforting, and I think if it were not for the fact that I had not had any breakfast I would have been tempted to turn over and go back to sleep. As I shifted in my chair, I heard a very familiar voice.

"Good morning, sleepy head. How was your morning nap, *Dad!*" The infliction on "Dad" did not sound endearing at all, so I knew before I opened my eyes I was in trouble.

Dad. Oh boy. My second thought came quickly but reluctantly. Leia was here and she was not happy. As I looked over at her, I could tell she was unsure how to react, likely because she wasn't sure how I was doing.

"Hi, kid," I said, sitting up and rubbing my eyes. "What are you doing here?" I tried to look surprised and composed at the same time.

Leia answered sternly, "What am I *doing* here? Seriously?"

"I mean, how did you know I was here?" I felt sheepish.

"When I didn't hear from you, I called your station and did my own detective work."

I should have known it would not take her long to figure out I was not home for a few days. She had my schedule and knew that if I wasn't home, I would be at work. I usually check in with her by phone every few days at least, usually more frequently, and we talk often by text, so I knew this lecture was coming, and it should not have been a big surprise to see her. "I guess you learned a little too much from your dad," I answered, smiling.

Leia's concern now came to the surface. "How are you feeling? Dad, what's going on? I need some information here. I want to be mad at you for not calling me right away, but I will wait. Right now you need to fill me in."

"Okay, okay, calm down. I will explain." I sat up so I could face my daughter. "Monday afternoon I was at a fire scene when I started to feel a little strange. I thought I was speaking normally but apparently, I was not, and a bit after that I passed out. Next thing I knew, I woke up in the hospital. That was about it. I wasn't sure what had happened to me right away and I couldn't speak very well when I woke up, so I decided to wait before calling you." I saw some of the anger leave her face. "One of the doctors stopped by to see me and told me I had had a minor circulatory event in my brain and that I should be up and out of here in the next few days. I also did not call you right away because there was no need for you to worry. And I wanted to make sure I knew everything before calling you."

"But..."

I stopped her before she could continue. "Leia, just a minute there. Before you yell at me you should know that I was planning on giving you a call when I woke up from this nap, honestly."

"Dad, if you had a supposedly 'minor circulatory event,' why would you be in the ICU? Is there more that you're not telling me?" She still had a concerned look on her face.

153

She was too smart, but I kept at my little white lie because I knew she would want to believe it. "Leia, when I was first brought in, they didn't know how things were going to be so they sent me up here just to be sure. It was just a precaution and as you can tell," I indicated my body in general, "I'm quite fine."

"I guess... Can I bring you anything? Do you need anything?"

I reassured her. "No, honey, I'm good. As I said, I don't expect to be here too long, so there's not much I need. I should be back home in a day or two. If it will make you feel better, how about when they let me out of here you pick me up and come and stay over a few days and you can see for yourself." I mentioned this because I really did not want to be alone when I got home—I was a little, well, concerned—and I knew it would make her feel much better too.

"Thanks, Dad. That would make me feel better and I'm sure you could use a hand around the house. How much longer are you going to be here?"

"I'm not sure yet, but you know me—I would like to get out of here as soon as possible. How about we go grab a coffee and some lunch, since I missed breakfast, and we can chat about it?"

"Sounds good. I will let the nurse know we are going for a stroll," Leia said as she got out of her chair.

After lunch I sent Leia on her way. I knew that if I let her, she would stay, but I was sure she had better things to do than to sit around at the hospital with me doing nothing. Thankfully she didn't question me too much about the nature of my "minor circulatory issue." I knew she would do that later, but I was also certain she was smart enough to figure out that it was a stroke, but for now she let it slide.

As I thought about Leia with a smile, I made my way back to my room. My smile disappeared when I stepped into the room because the bed next to mine, where the woman had been, was now empty. There had been a commotion in the room around breakfast time, hence my stay in the lounge and missing that meal, and I had then been downstairs with Leia for a couple of hours, so I didn't see the end of the incident. I figured it was a good thing for Leia not to have witnessed whatever happened. I had spent twenty-two years protecting her and insulating her from the bad things in the world.

I also noticed that the gentlemen with the beard was not in the room, but his quilt was still on his bed. His absence confirmed my belief that I had seen him, and a woman I assumed was his wife, down in the cafeteria. I thought it was a good sign that he was up and about like I was.

However, the heavy-set man was still in the room and still appeared to be in a deep sleep. I was not a stroke expert but it seemed that from this small sample size—just the patients in my room—the ones who were up and about seemed to be the ones getting out of here and with pretty good function. I wondered if that was normal.

I was still standing in the doorway when a voice called to me. It was Dr. White. I turned to see she was just wrapping up a conversation. She motioned as if she wanted to have a quick chat with me, so I waited at the doorway. She approached briskly and said, "How are things this today, Detective? I imagined you would be up and about today and I'm glad to see I was right." She motioned for me to have seat on my bed. "How are you feeling?"

As I sat down, I thought about the question for a moment and then said, "I'm feeling much better today. I still have some tingling and a bit of a headache this morning but otherwise I am feeling pretty good."

"Excellent. I'm glad to hear it. I want to send you for a quick CT this afternoon just to have a look and make sure everything is flowing well and we have no new bleeds occurring."

"Okay, sounds good. If there is a bleed, we have an option to treat it, I presume?"

"Yes, we would have a couple of options but I'm hoping there are no new issues at this point and that this will turn out to be just a precautionary scan. I know I can be straightforward with you. If there is a bleed, it could be a major issue and could mean surgery, or worse. But based on your movement today I think you should be okay. I genuinely don't think there will be any new issues. You look and sound well. The lingering issues you describe are common and should subside."

"Okay," I replied with relief. Given that positive conversation, I thought this might be a good time to negotiate with the good doctor. "So given that I'm up and about and feeling well, and if the scan appears normal, I'm hoping I could go home tonight. What do you think?"

Dr. White looked like this conversation was something she was very used to. She folded her arms. "I'd like to wait and see." Damn. "I would also like to get you signed up for a research program in an effort to get you healthy, and keeping you here one more day will help that process stick."

I admitted defeat. "Okay. By the way, Dr. White, I caught some of your lecture this morning. Very interesting, though obviously I didn't fully understand all the information. But what I did gather was that this place is pretty novel in its approach and the application of research to practice is really important. I wanted to say good job. It was convincing information and seems like real change that can be done with the right people in place. Is this process being implemented as a standard approach throughout the country?"

Dr. White smiled and replied, "Well... the hospital world is not that quick at adapting to change, and one of the major stumbling blocks is the cost of running a program like this one. Of course, the human cost of *not* running a program like this is quite high as well. I'm glad you enjoyed the lecture. Which brings me to the research programs we having running right now and which I'm hoping I can get you connected with as soon as today. I have one of our researchers coming in to give some information to your roommate, Mr. Batton," she indicated the bed where the bearded man resided, "very shortly and I was hoping I could get you to head down to the games room and listen. I think you would benefit from the activities and the research. In addition, you can be moved over after discharge to the research program and continue to receive scans of your brain as part of the program, and they're difficult to get unless you're in a dedicated stream, as you are right now."

I thought about what Dr. White was telling me. She made some excellent points. "No doubt I'm going to be off work for a little while. A free look at my brain would certainly be helpful if I have any further issues. Plus, why would I not want to make sure I'm fully recovered as soon as possible? It's a no brainer." I winked. "So it sounds like an excellent idea. I like the idea of the program. Plus, I already had a brief stop at your games room this morning to try out a video game. It was a lot of fun and I would certainly be interested in being the best I can post-recovery, so sign me up."

"Excellent. If you can head down to the games room now, Dr. Stern should be there shortly and she can provide you with an overview of the program. After that I'll have one of the nurses collect you to get your scan done, and I'll let you know how things look."

"Thank you, doctor." With that, she hurried down the hall. I was certainly interested in hearing more about the research being conducted. Again, I was left wondering about so many other individuals not having access to this type of program or this type of hospital. What did those people do? I was guessing their recovery was not the same, and their care was not the same. Maybe they ended up with long-term issues, which I thought was pretty sad. I felt so fortunate to be receiving such great care, though it was pretty much the luck of the draw, being in the right hospital at the right time. I realized the parallels between this and police work, which relied a lot on being in the right place at the right time. So much of the information we received, so many of the cases we broke, came down to being in the right place at the right time.

I made my way down the hall to the nursing station. "Dr. White said I would be having a CT scan today, so just to let you know where I am, so you can come and collect me, I'll be in the games room."

As I continued down the hall, I thought about a recent case that ended up being all about being in the right place at the right time. I'm sure that happens in all types of work, and maybe it has more to do with being available and ready to help. Police are often in the right place at the right time because we strive to be in the right spots. So it's not always by luck.

But some days it is. A few weeks ago, most of my shift decided to go out for breakfast. Our breakfast place of choice was right across the street from a bank. There were about twelve of us having breakfast when a call came over the radio for a robbery in progress—at the bank across the street. So we all rushed out, pulling our cars literally a few yards out of the parking lot to block the street. I'm not sure how the robbers missed them, but there were four marked cars in the lot when they went into the bank. It pays to pay attention to detail!

We quickly set up to cover all the exits and when they stepped out of the bank minutes later, we were waiting. Surprise! I'm sure they hadn't anticipated that kind of police response time! We quickly surrounded the four of them. One dropped his weapon right away and put his hands in the air; another lay down on the ground. He was carrying two large bags. The others, however, were closer to their car and started to shoot in an attempt to escape. That turned out to be a bad idea. Two of our officers had ready C8 carbine rifles. One robber was killed and the other wounded badly. We were just in the right place at the right time.

As I thought of the damage a body could sustain when hit by a C8 round I began to assess my own physical ability. I was still feeling a bit weak on my right side, though I was able to hide it. I was also able to hide the slight visual neglect I was experiencing; neither of these deficits was significant enough for someone to notice, and I was not about to show my weaknesses. I knew that a visual deficit might cause a physician to take my driver's license away, and with good reason. But my feeling was that it was not that big of a detriment to my ability to drive, especially when you consider that some individuals with perfect vision can't seem to get from A to B without cutting people off, mounting curbs, and going through red lights.

But not being able to drive would create such isolation for me, and I'm sure many other people would think the same way. My independence would be, to a certain extent, taken away, and that would be devastating. What do people do who live where there is no transportation if this happens to them? The isolation and loss of independence would be very depressing. If I were in that position, I'm not sure what I would do. If you have no support system, you become reliant on others. I'm certain such a situation would cause a person to age prematurely. They'd be less active, and spend their days doing what? I'm sure I would be drinking every day, sitting in front of the TV, watching the world from my living room but not being a part of it. I spent enough time inside my own head right now; I could only imagine how bad it would be if I were isolated.

But I wasn't, and I was thankful for that. I was going to get on track, and I'd be fine. Plus, when I got home, I would have Leia waiting for me, which made me very happy.

As I rounded the doorway to the rehab/games room I saw the man from the bed across from me. I didn't really know him, but it was still nice to see a familiar face, to see that he was up, and to know he was interested in the same program I was. I thought I better introduce myself.

CHAPTER 11
THE ROAD TO RECOVERY

Thomas and Ella were in the games room having a look at the set-up there. Colourful posters on the walls described recent research at the hospital, including work by researchers involved in the stroke recovery program. Some of the images were quite convincing, showing scans of the brains of individuals before and after going through the training program, with captions explaining that the differences in colour meant changes in the amount of brain activity.

Thomas's enthusiasm was tempered, however, by his feeling that researchers would pick truly exceptional examples to make their point and support their conclusions. Thomas also knew from his extensive reading that sample size was a significant factor influencing overall results, so he always made a point of checking the number of individuals involved in any study; one example didn't mean much. He also knew that whether the sample was big or small, the statistical significance of any result needed to be examined closely to get a true understanding of whether the results were meaningful, and thus understanding effect size was truly essential.

Ella pointed out the table tennis game. "We should try a few games, see if we still have the knack." They had had a table at home but had parted ways with it long ago to reclaim the space it occupied.

"Pretty sure I'm still terrible." Thomas was intrigued by the arcade games and interested in their role in stroke patients' recovery, most importantly his recovery. He also noticed a stack of board games and, happily, a chessboard. He didn't get to play chess often because Ella was not much of a fan, but he was hoping he would get a few games in while he was here. Maybe one of the other patients played.

Today seemed to be Day 1 of recovery. Though Thomas was feeling much better, his strength was not all it should be. And though he had not mentioned it to anyone yet, he was certain that he had lost a lot of the feeling in his left hand. As they looked around Thomas recognized the gentlemen from the opposite side of his room coming through the door.

***

As I entered the room, I immediately noticed the man from the bed across the room. I was happy to see that he was also up and about. I crossed the room and introduced myself. I believed it was important to give a genuine hello to the people I meet. I find it often makes my job easier. And, it would be plain impolite not to address the others in the room, especially since they were roommates. "Declan Myles," I said, shaking Thomas's hand.

"Thomas Batton. And this is my wife, Ella." We shook hands.

"Any chance you are the maker of that lovely quilt?"

Ella blushed and answered, oddly enough, with "Guilty as charged."

"I guess we're both in here for the same thing, Glad to see you're doing well." I said.

"Yes, I guess we are," Thomas said. "Not sure about the others in the room, though. Haven't seen them up yet. How have you been finding it here?"

"It's been really good, all things considered. But from what I understand, the kind of care we're getting, things like this room, isn't what it's like everywhere. It's too bad this kind of care seems to be limited, and depends on the hospital, or what city you're in when you end up having a stroke. I guess we *are* pretty lucky, if you can say that about having a stroke, that we made it to Lakefield General." I replied.

A woman holding a clipboard entered the room. Thomas and I studied her as she crossed the room. She was tall and thin, with long red hair bound in a braid. She wore a black blazer over a white blouse with a black pencil skirt and a black sports watch. She pulled a chair up to the table where Thomas, Ella, and I were sitting and set her clipboard down.

"Hello. I'm Dr. Gwen Stern. You are Detective Myles and Mr. and Mrs. Batton, correct?"

Thomas and I both replied, "Yes." On hearing "Detective," Thomas and Ella exchanged a very discrete glance, but I noticed.

"Great. I'm glad you're both up and out of your rooms. I take that as a really good sign," said Dr. Stern. "So, I'm a neuroscientist working out of the local university. I'm a professor there and also one of the primary researchers on the stroke wing, and I spend most of my time here working on a number of projects. My current major project is studying the degree and speed of recovery of stroke patients using an interactive cognitive training program to assist with standard post-stroke care. So as part of that, I'd like to ask you some questions. First, do you mind having this discussion together? Because we can, of course, do it privately if you prefer."

"I'm fine with a group interview," I said.

"Fine for me too," said Thomas.

"Great. Having more people does tend to lead to better discussion. So first question, what are your major concerns right now?"

Thomas spoke first. "Well, I believe my major concern is whether I'm going to be able to do everything I could do before. And I guess I would be concerned that I may have another stroke and that my brain and body won't be okay next time. I guess I'm just hoping to return to my status quo."

Pointing to my own head, I added, "I certainly agree with that. My concern is that everything up here is going to work as it once did. I really rely on being able to solve complex problems and if my brain isn't working right... well... that would be a real concern. But at the moment it seems intact and I would like to keep it that way."

Dr. Stern made some notes and nodded. "That's exactly the point I've been trying to get across to many people working in my field. The brain is the base of *everything*, and if you want to walk right, speak well, and solve problems, then what needs to be working well is your brain. But the general course of hospital rehabilitation, unfortunately, has been to get individuals access to overworked speech therapists and occupational therapists first. The hospital wants individuals to be able to speak and care for themselves, and as soon as that happens you can be discharged.

"But research, here and elsewhere, shows that early discharge creates high re-admission rates: people who go home too early may end up spending more time in the hospital later on. In addition, we've found that neglecting to offer care beyond traditional methods leaves more deficits than you would see in people that had received greater attention. This is a general statement for many illnesses, actually. History suggests that greater attention to the patient can improve the level of recovery significantly.

"So if the brain is damaged, and if it's the most important part of functioning as a whole, then if we're going to spend time with any part of the body should this not include a significant amount of time working on getting your brains better? For stroke patients specifically, I'm concerned about secondary consequences, such as another stroke within a few months of discharge and ongoing deficits, which can turn into lifelong deficits. Other concerns include whether we can speed up recovery and ensure minimal concerns going forward. So with all these things in mind, my idea is that we need to train the brain, the injured organ, as soon as we can and as comprehensively as we can."

The three listening could tell as Dr. Stern spoke that she was passionate about her work. As she spoke, she became very animated and appeared intensely concerned about things that needed to be done but were obviously not being done, or done in a way she wished they were done. She continued. "Very often, occupational therapists believe they're adding cognitive training to their programs, thus covering off brain training, but the extent and type of training are well short of what I believe needs to be done. Don't get me wrong—we need our occupational therapists and they do important work—but they have limited knowledge of the brain's mechanisms, especially in relation to brain recovery."

Dr. Stern gave them a moment to take in what she'd said and then continued. "The goal of my research here in the stroke wing is to get to patients as soon as I can, simply because we know that the brain is undergoing a reorganization and a restructuring, so to speak, after injury and I want to facilitate this reorganization by increasing the brain's connectivity to enable better or even different connectivity. Researchers have known for many years that the areas of the brain do not work in isolation and we are beginning to understand the heightened level of connectivity and shared resources used between brain regions to complete even the most mundane tasks. Some primary bundles of neurons— nerves—connect large areas of the brain from one region to other regions."

Dr. Stern stood and went to one of the posters to point out regions of the brain. "Some of those regions are the inferior longitudinal fasciculus, the inferior occipitofrontal fasciculus, and the posterior thalamic radiation. These are some great examples of bundles of neurons that we know are involved with linking several brain regions that assist in preforming numerous tasks, including normal everyday things like crossing the street or making a cup of tea. Connectivity of regions is essential to do those things. With crossing the street, for example, there are a bunch of calculations your brain does to perform what we see as an everyday, routine task. But if you look more deeply, we need to be able to track the speed of cars in both lanes of traffic, check the traffic signals or note where stop signs are, watch for cars making left or right turns, looking for bicycles, anticipating cars disobeying the rules of the road, and so on. Even common tasks use numerous brain resources and require input from various brain regions working together to track objects and safely navigate from one side of the street to the other.

"The goal of my training program is to make sure we activate the entire brain and strengthen connectivity, and maybe provide new routes when old routes are not available anymore. And just so you know, if you've ever heard that we only use 10% of our brain," Dr. Stern shook her head. "This couldn't be further from the truth, as you can see from those areas I just pointed out. Even at rest we use several regions of our brains, so that 10% thing really bugs me.

"Anyway! I'm sure you're wondering why we're basically in a mini-arcade. And the answer is not because my post-docs think it's cool, though people wonder sometimes if that's actually why it's here, since they take a lot of breaks in this room. No, the reason is that I'm a firm believer in using visuomotor control activities as much as possible to assist people who've had strokes. I like these activities because an area of the brain called the posterior parietal cortex is highly active when patients are doing tasks such as tracking objects and when they move toward a target. We can see that from functional MRIs and electroenceph-alograms. This area is sort of at the top and back of your head," she said, placing her hand on the top of her head slightly towards the back, "and it's linked to a number of other areas in the brain. When tasks become more complex, as they do in these games, the more resources are needed, and doing that kind of task leads to better integration from other brain areas."

Dr. Stern paused and smiled. "If you're brain's about to implode from information overload I just provided let me know."

"I think I follow," I said, "more or less".

"Carry on," said Thomas.

"One of the primary games I use in my research is Pac-Man. I use Pac-Man because it requires numerous brain regions to talk to each other to successfully progress through the game. Though on the surface it appears to be just a game, from a neuroscientist's point of view it's a challenging task for the brain. For example, the posterior parietal cortex, the PPC, becomes active when you begin to track the location of items in the game, such as the moving ghost, Pac-Man's progress, etc. As well, to see the objects in the first place the visual cortex needs to be active, and visual information is transferred through a few other brain regions and then to the PPC to assist with navigation. The game also requires you to clear the board, so you need a strategy to get around, and that means getting assistance from the frontal regions to help with decision-making, including specialized assistance from the dorsal lateral pre-frontal cortex." She pointed this out on the brain diagram.

"So that's a lot of brain resources already at work, but in addition, you have to activate motor regions of your brain and send signals through the brainstem to your muscles to move the joystick. There's also the need to navigate on a vertical screen using a joystick that's on a horizontal plane, which is an additional element of organization for the brain to complete. The game is also ideal because as you get more efficient, the level of difficulty increases automatically." She paused briefly then added ... "And you thought you were just wasting your time in the eighties."

"I'd like you to call my mom and tell her that, if you wouldn't mind," I said with a chuckle.

She didn't respond and but continued on. "With all these resources at work, the goal is to develop recovery through continued brain activation or modification or however you wish to think of it. In addition to the arcade games we've also developed other tasks aimed at increasing brain activity. Though, as I said, brain areas never work in isolation, we do focus on different types of tasks that will more heavily tax one area versus another to ensure we're activating as many areas as possible. If required we can add more activities to help activate areas that might need more attention. Other activities include the language center, the navigation center, the design center, and a few others I'll review as we train.

"Your training will take place for two hours a day, every day you're in the hospital, and then, once you're discharged, we'll work for two hours a day, three days a week. This will be in conjunction with take-home tasks. We will keep you in the program for ten weeks, include pre-assessment and post-assessment. Again, I'll describe these elements as we move along."

"So when do we start," I asked.

"To start training I'll need informed and voluntary consent from each of you, if you're willing to start the program."

"I'm in," said Thomas.

"I should also let you know that you can drop out at any time, no explanation required. In addition, because you'll be off site shortly you will, of course, need to get to the training. So to make sure you can get here, instead of you having to worry about transportation, we'll provide you both with cab vouchers and you can just pass those to the drivers. This way you won't have to worry about parking, either, which is a huge cost for everyone, especially if you work here; trust me. I have forms here for you to sign if you're interested and an information sheet for you to read over as well, which should answer any further questions you might have."

Dr. Stern handed the forms to Thomas and me. As we reviewed them, she said, "There are varying levels of functionality in patients in the program, and we have a staff of two post-doc students, three graduate students, two research assistants, two undergrad volunteers, and a lab manager to assist in program delivery." She stopped talking to let us tend to the paperwork.

Dr. Stern thought that both of these patients seemed like great candidates for the program. Though they appeared to have had good recoveries so far she was sure she could get them even healthier. She could help a lot of people if they just committed to the program.

Both men understood the importance of ensuring that what you were signing was what had been explained to you, so they read things over carefully. As they read, Ella asked a question. "Dr. Stern, I'm just wondering, if you don't mind me asking, what kind of success the program is having. Are you seeing positive results?"

"That's an important question, Mrs. Batton. The program is still very much in the early stages in relation to seeing long-term changes so it's difficult to talk about results at the moment, but for the short time, about ten months, that we've been delivering the program it's been working quite well. I can tell you the individuals that have been put through it so far have been very successful in their recovery, so much so that at this hospital I will approach everyone who has had a stroke or other brain injury and explain the benefits we have seen and offer them an opportunity to join. We even stopped using a portion of our patients as a control group, meaning they would just get standard treatment, because of how effective the program appears to be. It would have been unethical to continue excluding some individuals from this treatment. The controls I'm now using come from a different hospital where access to the program isn't feasible at this time."

When I heard this, it solidified my theory of what happens to people who aren't lucky enough to be in a place like this. Those people could end up with lifelong deficits simply because there was no access to the same treatment I was about to receive. I wondered why this program was not being rolled out on a bigger scale. As I tried to reconcile the information I'd just heard with what I thought *should* be happening, it seemed that the puzzled "working out a problem" look I was known for developed on my face. Dr. Stern noticed.

"Are you okay, Detective?"

"I'm just trying to understand everything, about the program I mean. Correct me if I'm wrong but from what I have surmised, apparently stroke patients, for the most part, are not engaged, or challenged, or—forgive me— cared for to the extent that they could be to help them recover more fully." I paused for a moment to gather the remainder of my thoughts on the subject. "So there appears to be a gap in care, and the brain is overlooked. Is that fair to say, doctor?"

"Well, I hope it's not as bleak as you present it, but I will admit there is a gap in care, and I'm trying to fill that gap and provide information to as many hospitals and institutions as I can, and let them know there are options and we can do better. I'm convinced that people are doing as much as they can with what they have, but there may be a more cost-effective, more efficient way for us to assist stroke patients in recovery. And not just to assist them but to make them *much* healthier. Society as a whole, and especially scientists and clinicians, need proof, and as scientists we need to prove over and over again that this really works, or that it's really happening. I believe whole-heartedly in this program and I will take every opportunity and every effort to show that what we're doing here really works."

I nodded. "I see what you're saying, but when you have all this knowledge and you find these great results and you know it can change lives, it must be difficult for you to present all this information and then have to prove it over and over again to get people to listen, no?"

"Let me answer that question with a question, which I promise not to do again. I assume that in your work as a detective you have come across a lot of individuals that you know are dangerous or have committed some terrible crime. I would also assume that sometimes there is a limited amount of evidence that you have, or that you can legally use in court. I know the result can sometimes be failure to get a conviction, even though you *know* an individual is guilty and you've made every effort to get the court to listen to your information. Do you give up?" Dr. Stern paused, and then simply stated, "I'm guessing that you don't, and how you answer that question would be how I would answer *your* question."

My first thought was, "damn doctors and their thoughtful insights, their ability to turn the tables on you; I hate that." My second thought was that she was totally right. The way I went about my work without going crazy was by trying to do my job to the best of my ability and provide all the information I could, all the evidence I could, and to make every effort to ensure the prosecution understood the case and what we know and what we can prove. At the end of the day, I could not get personally attached to cases, or at least I certainly tried not to, because I knew I could only control my own actions and contributions. Beyond that, I had to let go of everything in the end. But when it went well and things worked out, it was a great feeling. I looked at Dr. Stern and nodded. "I get it, trust me." I wanted to learn everything about her work to help stroke patients.

After reading through the material, Thomas and I signed the paperwork. During this process I came to see that Thomas was a highly intelligent man who chose his words wisely and said what he meant and meant what he said. I also got the feeling that Ella and Thomas were really good people, and it was nice to meet people like that, regardless of where and why we were where we were.

Dr. Stern spoke a little more about the logistics of the program and reviewed the training schedule. "We can even get started tonight after dinner." We agreed. I figured that since we knew we would be discharged soon, it would be good to start as soon as possible to get an idea of the things we might be doing. Dr. Stern was pleased we were ready to start and told us that one or both of her post-doc fellows would run us through the program tonight to ensure we were on track. "Since the hospital always wants to feed you at about 4:30, it shouldn't be a problem to be here for 6:00 PM. Okay?" With that set and the documents signed, Dr. Stern was off.

Thomas, Ella, and I sat for a moment after she left and engaged in the usual chat of people who have just met. But not long into the conversation a nurse arrived to let me know they were ready for my CT scan. "So I guess I'll see you a bit later," I said, and went with the nurse for one of the many brain scans to come.

CHAPTER 12
REBUILDING THE BRAIN

On my way back from my scan I longed for something warmer to wear. It was cold in here! I thought I would give Leia a call and have her bring me some clothes, including a hoodie or something similarly cozy. The CT scan had gone quickly. In fact, the technician had arrived just as I arrived; they obviously have this timed out to the minute. I was certainly happy that I hadn't had to wait.

As I passed the nursing station, Sarah let me know that dinner would be up in a little while. "Great!" What I meant was, "Pass me the phone—I need to order pizza."

As I entered my room, I noticed straight off that the woman who had been in the bed to my right wasn't there. My first thought was that we were in the ICU and she certainly had not been up and about, so there seemed to be only one logical place where she had gone from here. The earlier medical emergency that kept me out of the room added to my grim thoughts. I gave myself an imaginary pat on the back, saying in my mind, "Fairly good detecting, Detective. You should tell your co-workers that your skills are still top notch." Which I was sure would give them all a good laugh. Perhaps the woman had just been taken for a scan. But then I realized the machines that had surrounded her bed were gone too.

I looked to the other side of the room and saw that the big man was now hooked up to a ventilator, not a good sign. It made a subtle whooshing sound every few seconds.

The absence of a roommate left me reflecting on how lucky I actually was that I was still here, with all my thoughts and feelings. Those feelings were difficult to reconcile at this point or even get a good handle on. I was beginning to understand how people say that unless you have come close to actually no longer existing, you don't really get it. Death is such a regular event in my line of work, but it would be hard to find anyone at work really reflecting on life or the fragility of our existence.

I remembered reading once how phenomenal it really is that we are even here on Earth at all, and how so many things in the universe had to go just right for us to even exist. For example, we just happen to be the right distance from the sun; any closer or farther away and no life would exist on this planet. But just being the right distance from the sun doesn't help unless the atmosphere develops in a way to allow the development of life. That humans have evolved to allow us to adapt to our environment and thrive when so many other species have not been able to is another remarkable feat. The curiosities of the world are countless, including such things as the existence of principles that can't be explained, such as how often the golden ratio, phi 1.618, occurs in the nature of the world. Is it all random? Kind of like my thoughts? No wonder I never reflect on life and death—as an investigator, where would I stop? I would just keep digging and digging. In the end, maybe it's better to just enjoy this existence than to question it.

I dug through my plastic bag of belongings to find my phone to call Leia to see if she could drop off something warm to snuggle up in, though when I talked to her I would find a more masculine term than "snuggle." I dreaded the thought of turning my phone on, since I knew that being in the new world where we text everything, I was bound to have two hundred messages wishing me well, which would no doubt include stupid messages from the guys showing "nurses" in sexy uniforms. I smiled in spite of myself.

Leia was happy to bring me some clothes this evening. I also let her know I was starting my training tonight and she was excited to see the program and what it consisted of. Though I was certainly a willing participant I also wanted to see Dr. White tonight because I wanted to know if I could go home. I guessed it would be tomorrow, based on the time of evening my training was to occur, and I felt they were more likely to discharge me the following day. My guess was that if she had looked at my CT scan yet, she was not in a rush to let me know how it turned out, though if it wasn't good, I'm sure I would have seen her by now. I could only assume all was well.

I finished my five-minute dinner of salmon, brown rice, broccoli—and Jell-O, of course. There was tea to drink, but I really wanted coffee. I had not been served a smaller meal since I was a child. I wondered if starvation was part of the training plan. I would be sure to ask. It appeared that Thomas had a similarly small meal, though he appeared to have some sort of pasta. Possibly. We remarked on the fine dining but kept it brief in consideration of the man in the other bed. I still had not seen him conscious, nor had I seen anyone visit him. But there had been a number of doctors looking at him and shaking their heads.

At 5:45 PM I got up and decided to make my way down the hall to the games room. I was a bit early but I could always get a game in before the trainers arrived. I was expecting Leia around 6:30 and I told her I would be here, so I was sure she wouldn't have difficulty finding me.

Thomas and Ella joined me on the stroll down the hall. We briefly talked about what had happened to us and how we got here. It made me feel better to know that someone understood exactly what I had gone through, in a way, though I was sure our experiences were still different in many ways.

Thomas and Ella seemed content to sit at the side of the room chatting to each other awaiting the trainer's arrival. I, however, was interested in playing a couple of games. I saw one of my favorites from when I was a kid, Galaga. I remembered spending a summer in the arcade playing this game for hours on end. When I stepped up to it, for a brief moment I felt like that kid again. Just without the hair hanging over my eyes, baseball cap on backwards, jean shorts, sandals, and the feeling of not having a care in the world. Back then quarters were a must, but now I pushed the button and the game sprang to life.

I remembered the game right away! Which guys to look out for, whether to let my ship be captured so I would do well at the challenge stages, or wait until later in the game—it all came back to me and for a moment I was lost in the game. I was doing really well when Dr. Stern came into the room with her two lab assistants, Molly and Erin.

"Good evening, gentlemen. I can see you are a both looking well and ready to go. Detective Myles, you seem to be the eager student tonight! This is Molly and Erin, my lab assistants, and they will be helping us over the next few weeks. In fact, they will stay with you throughout your training sessions. Both my post-doc students were busy tonight with other projects so I made sure to be here for your first session.

"Tonight," Dr. Stern continued as I stepped away from the game, "will start with an introductory session, and tomorrow morning we'll complete some neuropsychological assessments to get a baseline value for where we're at. The goal here is to focus on each area of the brain, though as I explained yesterday, that's with the clear understanding that brain areas don't work in isolation.

"Tomorrow morning, we'll also be doing MRIs on you, but that's just a resting examination to get a look at your default mode network to get an understanding of how your brains operate generally. It's quite common for researchers to examine brain networks in a resting state, and to then look for changes later down the road. Structural scans will be available for ongoing care, which is of a great benefit. Tonight's an introduction but we'll also be assessing your abilities."

By the time Dr. Stern had explained these details, Leia had arrived and was standing in the doorway. She had a bag with her. I motioned for her to come in, and I introduced her to everyone. When she sat down next to me, I realized it was really nice to have her here. As Dr. Stern continued, I opened the bag and found a big warm hoodie and pulled it on. It felt like the best piece of clothing I'd ever worn.

The first part of our assessment was visuomotor skills. Dr. Stern presented Thomas and me with tablets, which were loaded with different games designed to test our abilities and track our performance at completing basic tasks, or at least that's how it appeared to me. The games were scored automatically and the scores and other information uploaded to the researchers' database to track our performance, which I thought was really cool.

Each day we were not completing onsite training we were required to complete various other exercises, which were outlined on the tablet. Each module was laid out for each day of the week. The research assistants were able to view our training and could review and adjust the games as required, as well as respond to our questions and feedback. The tablets had an additional program that measured blood pressure and pulse, with plug-in assessment tools that assisted with these measurements. This data was also sent back to the central database.

Finally, the tablets contained a diary section in which Dr. Stern wanted us to record how we were feeling each day and provide comments and feedback as we progressed through the program. This all seemed to be very cutting edge and I was amazed at what they could do with these tools.

After Thomas and I played a few of the arcade games, with the lab assistants tracking a number of things, including scores, level reached, and time on the game, I asked Erin, "What's in there?" indicating the door marked Training Lab.

"Good question," she replied. "We're going there next. It's *very* cool."

Dr. Stern heard Erin answering the question and came over and opened the door. "Okay, gents, on to our next training area. Family members are welcome too."

As we all moved through the door I saw there were two large screens on opposite walls, each with a computer system nearby, with a visor attached. Dr. Stern explained that this lab used a number of different assessment tools. "But the one everyone focuses on is our virtual reality system. We're going to use the system for a number of different tasks. One is a wayfinding task, and this is where we put you in a maze and you have to find your way out. Another program we use for wayfinding is a city street program where you have to reach a destination.

"We also use memory tasks and matching tasks, which will be completed in virtual reality with a tablet system, but there are also pen-and-paper versions if the tablet becomes uncomfortable. These big screens will project what you're seeing in the visor and give the researchers a view of what you're seeing and doing. We can alter the program while it's in operation. Just to give you an example, one of the games involves building a pyramid where you can spin it around and place the blocks wherever you need them as it increases in size; it's a very spatial type of game."

I thought the tablet was cutting edge, but the virtual reality thing was on a whole new level.

Dr. Stern said, "Okay, so let's get you hooked up and see what you can do."

Leia remarked, "Looks pretty cool, Dad. Try not to puke!"

"Gee thanks." I was hoping she wouldn't notice the small visual problem I was experiencing. The large screen was going to project everything I did in this virtual world and I was feeling a bit apprehensive—I didn't want my daughter to see that there was anything wrong with me. I'm the dad and dads are strong and don't need help. I'm supposed to be the one who helps her. I'm supposed to be strong for her. But now, if there were any flaws in my performance she might begin to worry. I couldn't have that.

As I was getting hooked up, I said to the researchers, "I've never tried anything like this before. I think I'm going to try some different things out just to see how it all works. Just play around, you know?" I thought if I laid some groundwork in regards to how I was just going to be fooling around with it, if any problems showed up I could suggest the mistakes were part of learning the system and a result of just having fun with it.

Erin placed the visor on my head and checked the fit, including adjusting the focus of the lens to ensure everything was corrected for my level of vision. I thought this was a little strange, and I was sure that Thomas might be struggling, but I could hear him asking questions at every step of the process. He seemed to be very inquisitive, very interested in the whole process, and though he asked a lot of questions his tone was soft and complimentary, and Molly was thus at ease answering him. Listening to how many questions Thomas was able to ask without being thought of as aggressive, intrusive, or bothersome made me envious of his ability and I thought he would have made a great police partner. He would have been the ying to my yang. Thomas's ease with the whole process put me a bit more at ease as well.

After the visor was in place, we had large harnesses attached to our torsos. Again Thomas's curiosity revealed the reason. Molly explained, "It's a precaution. Because you're going to be on these big treadmills to mimic the walking you'll do in the virtual world, it can be disorienting and we don't want you to fall." This all seemed very elaborate and I found myself wanting to know how much all this equipment cost. I made a mental note to ask Dr. Stern at some point.

Dr. Stern added, "People who have recently had a stroke will often have problems with their gait and balance. There's ongoing pressure-sensitive measuring during this assessment, which will show us if you might be favoring one particular side over the other, which is helpful for the occupational therapist."

Dr. Stern explained further. "This type of task can be conducted around the hospital simply by giving a patient a map of the hospital and a destination. But the virtual reality system tracks a number of different things we can't examine in the real world. For example, we can track eye movements through the visor, which tells us where you're focusing and where you look and for how long, and we can compare that to a control group—people who aren't in this program. The differences can be used to help a patient to correct where and what they need to be concerned about in the real world.

"But using a map and finding a new area to navigate in the real world can also help patients recover because it activates essential brain areas." The amount of knowledge she was able to pass on in a few sentences was remarkable, very similar to Dr. White.

As I stepped on the treadmill and took a few steps, I found its speed would increase or decrease depending on how fast I walked. We were presented with two landscapes. One was a cityscape and the other a park landscape. Each contained a map, which we could refer to by looking down—it looked like it was projected in our hands. The cityscape came with pedestrians and traffic, all operating as they would in the real world. The map provided start and finish points, and had a star to show you where you were at any point, like the "you are here" on a map at a mall. I could see my speed and errors, such as wrong turns. It was a remarkable experience.

In the cityscape, I needed to cross the street. But a car had just turned the corner and because of my new blind spot, I was... how should I put this... smoked by this car, which happened to be a taxi. I laughed it off. "I was wondering what would happen if I did that. I thought maybe the cars would stop. Great system, Doc—just what you'd expect in the real world!"

I was hoping my comment would cover up the fact that I was having trouble seeing things in the lower right-hand side of my visual field. It wasn't a huge spot but when you know something should be there and it's not, it's difficult to get used to. Sometime during my next few sessions, when Leia was not around, I would talk it over with Dr. Stern and Erin and see if there were things we could do to fix this.

Thomas and I continued to try various navigation routes and played a few of the games, but after about thirty minutes we were both exhausted. The researchers, I think, were attuned to our body language and knew right when to shut it down.

As we were getting out of our harnesses, Dr. Stern said, "I'd like you to take some time tonight to write some comments about the program in the journal area on your tablets. If you open them up now I'll walk you through it." Thomas and I sat down and turned our tablets on. Dr. Stern showed us how to use the diary. It actually had two sections, one called "open" and the other called "private." "Our researchers have access to entries in the open section and will read your notes there and respond to any questions. From there they can alter the program as needed or just make notes for further program development.

"The private area is where we encourage you to write whatever you want. If you hate your training and you don't want to tell us, write it here—although we'd rather that you told us if that's the case. If you're frustrated about something and need to get it out and down somewhere, write it here. We know from other patients that it's very useful to have an area where you can vent about anything you want, anything at all, and it doesn't need to be about what's happening right now with the training, it can be anything. Some patients, once they've recovered, actually transfer their content from this area to the open area, which has been very helpful for us in structuring this program effectively. However, the control is yours. You can delete this content anytime you wish, or leave it forever. Well, not forever. After ten years it will be erased automatically, so if you wrote a book or something in this area make sure you transfer it out before ten years are up. We had to include the auto-erase feature to get it through our ethics committee." Thomas and I poked at our tablets, trying things out.

Dr. Stern continued. "Thank you for the great work tonight. You did really well. I know you're exhausted but please know your work will pay off in the long run. I will see you tomorrow for more." I thought, well, they may see me tomorrow for a brief follow-up, but I was certainly not staying in the hospital another night after tonight, that was for sure.

On our way back to my room Leia and I stopped at the lounge to chat. I told her, "I spoke with Dr. White and she said I would be heading home tomorrow, though I will, of course, be around for my scans and my training. But I will not be sleeping here or eating 'dinner' here again." Leia could see I was determined to go, but I think she also knew that for someone like me it was best that I was out of here anyway.

"I'll come by late tomorrow afternoon and pick you up. And like I said, I will be staying with you for a few days, just in case."

I laughed and replied, "Of course, honey. I'm happy to have you anytime and you can stay as long as you want." We stood and I gave her a big hug. "And thanks for bringing me the clothes. I'll see you tomorrow. I'm going to sit here for a bit and work on my new diary."

"Dear Diary, my daughter's the best," Leia said. She gave me a kiss on the cheek and headed down the hall, waving over her shoulder as she left.

I sat staring at the blank screen of my tablet. I thought about Dr. Stern's comment about writing a book in this space. How cool would that be? But I didn't think I was going to start that journey tonight. I was feeling a little melancholy now that Leia had left, maybe because I knew no one else was coming to see me anytime soon and nobody was coming to see me when I got home, either. In the cop world, if you're sick, you're out of sight and sort of out of mind. I trusted each one of my colleagues with my life when I was there, but weakness is not something any cop deals with well. But that's okay because we all understand that's how it is.

I still didn't know what to put on my first page. Eventually I wrote, "I am okay, I will be okay, and things will get better." Then I added a title for the next paragraph:

To Do List

- Get brain back to 100%, including vision.
- Keep in good shape because it's important for recovery (of anything).
- Help those that cannot help themselves.
- Be a better person.
- Get my affairs in order.
- Find a sole mate.

A blue squiggly line appeared under "sole mate." I looked at it for a moment and then had a laugh. I wondered if my misspelling was a message in and of itself, but I hoped not.

I thought of adding a number of other items to the list but then thought that if it became too long, I would never start. But I think making the list was a good exercise and I would recommend that everyone sit down and make list of big things to do in their life. I felt like it provided me with some short-term focus and maybe also some long-term goals, especially the soulmate part. I knew I would be retiring from the force soon, and during transitions it is important to refocus. I wondered if many people my age had the same type of thoughts.

I looked around, and listened. The hospital sure was a quiet, lonely place at night; I could not imagine being here for long period. There were so many people rushing around during the day, but at night it was a very different story. I think if I were here for a long time I would have to bring in my rollerblades and try them out in the halls at night.

I made another notation in my journal, this time on the open side. My comments were about how wonderful the program seemed and how noble the cause was that the researchers were trying to undertake. I also wondered about the people in this country and in other countries who did not have access to such an advanced program. Were these individuals to be punished for the lack of access to resources? And if that was the case, why was it the case? If the program was here, and working so well, why not expand it to regions that required assistance? What was being done, what could be done, to help other individuals who strokes? I was by no means suggesting a revolution in the healthcare system, but certainly something more must be done. And if it wasn't, why not? Of course, as Dr. White said in her lecture, economics certainly had its role, but something so fundamental could be rolled out without a significant effort, could it not?

I was really tired after forming all these thoughts and ranting on my diary page. I wanted to get some rest, though I longed for it to be in my own bed. I would be sure to bring up my departure with Dr. White tomorrow because there was not a chance I was staying here one more day. I would make that clear tomorrow, but I believed we were on the same page. I paused for a moment before I hit the Save and Submit buttons on the program, but I was sure the comments were valid and hopefully inspiring. As I made my way out of the lounge, I passed the nursing station and commented how quiet it was here at night.

The nurses at the desk agreed. Jeffrey said, "It's more noticeable in the intensive care units than anywhere else. Sometimes I head off for a walk to a different area just to keep awake and remain social to some extent."

As I reached my bed I could see that Thomas was fast asleep. I was sure he was as tired as I was from this evening's activities. As I eased into my railed bed, I looked at the empty bed next to me, where the woman had been—it seemed just a short time ago, resting quietly with no urgent concerns. I wondered if she had slipped away peacefully and had no idea what was happening. Or was there a bright light, and was there anything at the end of it all? That's the ultimate question that can never be answered until you get there.

I believed religion offered people who were afraid of death something to help them handle their day-to-day reality. People often say things like, "it was their time," or "they're in a better place now." Religion was funny sometimes; it provided structure and in some cases a recipe for how to live beyond this existence: if you complete A you will reach B, and if you are frightened to live in the now, take comfort because in the end things will be okay; just keep toeing the line. The only alternative to this view was nothingness, and for more than half the world, if they truly believed there was nothing at the end of it all, they wouldn't know how to live now, what choices they should make. Would the world be different? Would societies be different?

These questions were too heavy for someone sitting in a hospital bed in an intensive care stroke ward. Then again, what better place to ask such questions than a hospital bed? I soon drifted off for some much-needed sleep.

***

I was awakened by a flash of light and a loud crack, like a tree breaking. Once I was semi-aware I realized it was, of course, a thunderstorm. It was unsettling, since when I first woke I forgot where I was.

Now that I was awake, I looked around and saw my two roommates, still fast asleep, lucky bastards. I wanted to go right back to sleep, but I'm so used to going right out the door to work after I wake up that I knew it would not be easy to fall asleep.

I needed to find something productive to do, so I got up. When I got to the nursing station I could see it was 3:45 AM. A nurse seated at the desk was working on the computer, and as she worked she took small sips from a large coffee cup. Her drink appeared to be a little too hot; she hesitated before each sip and blew across the top of the liquid, making tiny ripples. "Good morning," I said, startling her. "I'm sorry! I didn't mean give you a jolt."

"Good middle of the night, Detective. Trouble sleeping? Or can I help you with something?"

"Always trouble sleeping, but I'm okay. The storm woke me and I decided to get up for a bit to stretch my legs."

"No problem. Let me know if you need any help."

With that I was off down the hallway. I thought of stopping off in the lounge but there was nothing to do there but sit and I didn't want to do that. So I headed down to the games room. As I strolled down the hallway I looked out into the night through the big windows. I could see the storm was in full force and the wind was howling. I suddenly thought, gee I hope all my windows are closed at home, but I wasn't so sure. Oh well; I guess the least of my worries right now is a wet carpet.

As I entered the games room I heard a faint beep I hadn't noticed before. Must be the system they spoke of that tracks the amount of time we're in the room, though I guess you could come in here and just sit down if you wanted to fool the system. Leave it to a cop to think of a way around something, I thought, chuckling.

As I looked at the games, I thought wow, who knew I was helping my brain when I was a teenager? Funnily enough, I had heard on the news recently that new surgeons were often avid gamers. The news story focused on how the video game world is similar to surgery in many ways: many surgeries today are done through small incisions and doctors use monitors to see during the operation, which is, I guess, a bit like playing a video game. I'm sure that also allows them some detachment from the patient. I went to Galaga and pushed the button and it fired up right away. The same thought came back to me again: no quarters!

After I'd played for about twenty minutes, a young man dressed in scrubs came into the room, eating what appeared to be an energy bar. He was a little startled to see me, but quickly regained his composure. "Hey. How are things?"

"Good, despite being here. As well as can be expected."

"I didn't mean to disturbed you. I'm a neurology resident and I'm on call tonight. Just finished up with a patient and I have to go back and check on some others shortly, so I thought I'd pop in here and have a break, play some games."

"No problem; nice to have the company. It's so quiet here at nighttime," I said.

"I know. I make a point of not watching any of those scary movies set in a hospital at night when I am on shift." He laughed loudly.

We played and chatted, mainly about where we were in our games, our scores, the levels we reached, or awesome moves we'd made. I felt almost normal again, just having fun and hanging out, though a hospital gown and a hoodie would not be my first choice of attire for hanging out. But the hoodie did make me feel better.

The resident said, "If you don't mind me asking, what are you in for?" Like what you'd say in prison!

"Seems I've had a stroke."

"Who's your attending physician?"

"Dr. White."

"That's excellent," he said. "I'm really impressed with her. Really, you couldn't have done better than her, like, in the whole country." That was quite comforting to hear. After fifteen or twenty minutes, the young doctor bid me farewell and was gone.

I played for what I was sure was almost an hour. When I stopped, I realized the storm must have passed—I could not hear the thunder or the wind anymore. I stretched mightily and decided to go for a little walk around the wing to stretch my legs. Walking made me think of exercise. I did want to get in some exercise when I get home; I needed to check with Dr. White about what I could and could not do.

After my stroll I could see it was still the dead of night. It felt like that time during a nightshift when everyone is ready to pack it in and is just waiting for their relief to come on shift. I had always found that this time of night was when my brain would shut down, and I liked to find a place to put my feet up and rest my eyes. I never did have the ability to genuinely fall asleep on nightshift, so really all I could do was rest a little. But tonight I felt pretty awake despite the time, though I knew I should get back to bed and get some rest. But the walk felt good.

As I looked down at the hospital's main entrance from the large bay window above I could see a few cars coming and going. Makes you wonder who's moving around at this time of night. Where are they going, and what are they doing? I noticed there were a lot of leaves and various pieces of litter on the ground, a result of the storm. I noticed in the park area out front that some tree branches had come down as well, which was not a surprise; the wind had sounded strong.

Dawn was coming and I wanted to be in bed before the sun came up so hopefully I could get some sleep. I made my way back to my room and eased myself into bed as quietly as I could so as not to wake my roommates. I was now very tried again and sleep came quickly.

CHAPTER 13
HOPE AND REFLECTION

Soft music played in the background, and floral tributes lined the walls. The chapel was packed with police officers in dress uniforms, along with a piper and a drummer ready to play their role. A flag was draped over the coffin at the front of the room. Black satin curtains hung just behind the coffin, adding to the melancholy effect. On a mahogany table near the coffin stood two large photos in classic black frames, one of happier days with my family and the other showing me on a fishing trip down south with the guys many years ago: in the background was an endless sunset and the prize marlin I had just spent three hours reeling in. It had been one of the most exhausting, yet one of the best, days of my life.

Leia, crying softly and wearing a black pant suit and dark sunglasses, sat in the front pew with her mother, who was wearing a red silk dress. Next to her was my new police partner, Abigail, who was struggling to keep it together; every so often she dabbed her eyes with a white handkerchief. Suddenly there was a loud crack of thunder, and blinding flash of lighting came streaking through the roof, striking the coffin and setting it ablaze. As the flames began to rise from the coffin people ran for the exits in chaos.

What the...? I woke abruptly—in my hospital bed, next to the window, very much alive. I took a deep breath, sat up, and looked around. Okay. I knew where I was and what was going on. The storm had returned. But the dream was still unsettling. The funny part was that I was more upset at the service that was happening in the dream than I was about the fact that it was *my* funeral. Why would I be in a chapel like that? That service looked terrible to me. I think the excitement of the lightning and the fire was an improvement.

I did *not* want that type of service at all when I died. My family would have strict instructions about what was to happen with my service and it was not happening at a funeral home or a chapel or a church, that was for damn sure. I would talk to Leia today to make sure she knew that I was not going to a funeral home and that my service—party, really—was to be at my local pub. If that establishment wasn't there anymore, any good Irish pub would do. In addition, the drinks were to be on me all night long and everyone was ordered to dance, drink, and have a good time, because if there was a heaven that was exactly what I'd be doing there. Everyone likes a good party, and what better way to go out than to buy some rounds for your friends? That made me think I had better set up some designated drivers... nothing would be worse than having a great time and getting drunk at a wake and then getting killed going home; that would be brutal. I had better add some contingencies for that.

As I gathered myself, I saw that Thomas was awake and Ella was sitting next to him. Both had sections of the morning paper and both appeared to be quite engaged in their reading. It looked like a cool morning outside but of course it was hard to tell from inside. I longed to get home—today. I was going to make that clear in no uncertain terms. I preferred to leave on a good note, but if I had to, I would just sign myself out. As I had aged, I'd tried to become more prudent in my actions, but I was still prepared to take a stand when necessary.

"Breakfast," I heard as a heavy-set woman in pink scrubs and a hairnet entered the room with a trolley. She headed in Thomas's direction first, and he and Ella hurried to clear his bed table to receive his tray. Next came mine. What yummy creation was I going to get today? As she set it down and retreated from the room she added happily, "Enjoy, gentlemen."

"Thanks" was our reply in unison. She did not leave a tray for our unconscious roommate.

I looked down at the pale pink cafeteria tray and saw one hardboiled egg, a small bowl of oatmeal, dry toast, a small glass of OJ and a cup of very weak tea. Oh boy! Where do I begin with such a great meal? Both Thomas and I got to it quickly. It wouldn't be any better cold.

As I was finishing my five-minute breakfast, Sarah, the nurse, came into the room. In a big voice, she said, "Good morning, everyone. How are you feeling today?"

My immediate reply was, "Good enough to go home!"

Ella and Thomas both smiled. Thomas spoke up and in a careful tone said, "I'm feeling very well today, thank you. I hope—indeed, assume—that I will be discharged today as my condition appears to be stable and I'm feeling quite well. I can't speak for the detective, but he does seem well." He smiled at me.

I thought, and then replied "well said, Thomas, and thank you for including me in your response, which was better than mine. It would be nice to get out of here sooner rather than later."

"Dr. White has already stopped by briefly this morning to check your charts and she's planning on speaking to both of you today. I don't see a problem, but it will be up to her if you will be discharged today," Sarah replied carefully.

"But these can come out now." She moved to Thomas's IV machine and turned it off. She removed the port from his arm and taped a bandage over the little wound. She checked his blood pressure, pulse, oxygen levels, and whatever else they look at, and recorded everything on her tablet, which I assumed got uploaded in real time to his chart. She repeated the same process for me. She then checked all the readings of our silent neighbor. I heard her sigh quietly.

Just before she escaped the room, she asked if there was anything we needed. I shook my head no and Thomas said, "No, thank you, nurse."

After Sarah left, I turned on my tablet. I thought I might write a few things in my diary about how I was feeling, which was pretty good. I could also see my vital signs were well within the normal range and there was no need to keep me here any longer. That was my assessment, anyway. I opened the to-do list I had made last night. I wondered if it was maybe too ambitious. I guess that depends on how I interpreted what I meant by each item. Except for my soulmate search. I'm not sure there's room for much interpretation on that one.

Then again, a dog could be one's soulmate, right? That would at least help me complete my list. A puppy... that was a good idea. I'd always wanted a dog but when I was married my wife would never agree. And I never got one after we divorced because I was never home. Hmm... so maybe I *will* get a puppy when I get home. It would be good company. I made a list of puppy pros and cons in my private diary section.

When I was finished, I got up to stretch my legs. I overheard Thomas and Ella discussing going downstairs to get coffee. We all headed out the door at the same time.

As we approached the nursing station, I noticed Sarah talking to a woman and a teenage girl who looked very upset. We stopped to let the other nurse know we were going for a stroll, as Thomas put it. Caroline looked up from the chart she was working on and said, "Okay, no problem. Just to let you know I expect Dr. White back here in about hour and half and I believe she wants to speak with both of you about going home. Also, Dr. Stern scheduled a training session for you both just after lunch, so if you are discharged today, we should have everything ready to go by then—paperwork, medication list, training schedule, next appointments, follow-ups, home visits—whatever's required. I will print out a hard copy but everything will be uploaded to your tablet calendar so you can see it at a glance. This is a great benefit when you're in the training program; everything can be uploaded remotely and automatic reminders will pop up for appointments."

"That sounds like a great idea," I replied.

Thomas added, "Splendid."

I saw Sarah lead the two visitors into our room.

Thomas and Ella made their way to the elevators at the far end of the hall on their way to the coffee shop on the first floor. Thomas seemed to me to be a well-read individual, based on the fact that he was well spoken and of course one's occupation is often a good indication too, though not always. I was happy I had ended up in the same room as him. I think being alone or with someone who was obstinate would have made my stay much more unpleasant.

I decided to pop down to the lecture hall to see if anything was "playing" this morning. When I got to the noticeboard on the wall, I saw there was a presentation on post-traumatic stress disorder underway. That would be very interesting and worth catching, simply because so many first responders had PTSD. I was curious to know what was currently being done for people with the condition. I quietly slipped into the lecture, hoping my presence didn't catch anyone's attention or disturb the lecture in any way. Fortunately there was an open seat right by the door and I sat down without being noticed. This certainly wasn't high school, because you'd never find a seat at the back of the class there.

The lecturer was discussing neuroplasticity, according to the slide on the screen. "Our brains are plastic and thus can be altered by significant events in our life. For example, the brain is often altered during very traumatic events. Some individuals who experience PTSD have been subjected to such an overwhelming event that their brain is unable to process the information effectively, so they do not encode the event. Essentially, the event is so traumatic they can't make sense of it, so they can't store or catalog the information appropriately. The result is that the event seems to remain ever-present. And because the event is always at the forefront of their thoughts, they constantly experience it through memories and through persistent and unwanted thoughts about it. The individual will struggle to reconcile the event itself with their understanding of the world and more importantly of their own world. Because the event is ever-present, memories of it can be triggered by anything that may have been present during the event.

"For example, someone who was robbed at gunpoint in a store may have truly believed, during the event, that they were about to die. Any stimuli around them at that time become heightened, and they are in a state of constant hypervigilance. So say for instance that the gunman orders them on their knees and they feel the barrel of the gun touch the back of their head. The gunman tells them to close their eyes and pray. And just then the door buzzer goes off as someone enters the store and the gunman flees.

Hearing a buzzer similar to what they heard during the robbery could trigger the onset of these memories and feelings and, more importantly, the overwhelming fear and anxiety of the event. You can imagine that this individual may have difficulty at times (not always) entering places with that type of buzzer on the door. That's an overdrawn example of how PTSD can be triggered in normal situations.

However, even the subtlest of stimuli can trigger the individual to relive a traumatic event. And sometimes the reaction isn't perceived to be triggered by anything at all, which makes it difficult for family or friends to understand why it happened. PTSD can also be associated with a culmination of events rather than a single event. The events are usually situations that create a heightened state of stress for long periods. Examples might be responding to high-stress or dangerous situations over and over, such as police and paramedics do, or long periods of heightened vigilance, such as with air traffic controllers and soldiers.

When an individual re-experiences the traumatic event, they experience fear or anxiety almost at the level they did during the original event, each time the memory reappears. So, the individual's brain becomes altered, resulting in maladaptive neural wiring. As they continue to relive the events, their symptoms can be strengthened every time. They may continue to respond with now-irrational fear, and the brain strengthens these neuronal connections. This illness can be devastating to normal functioning. The question for researchers is to find ways to get the brain back on track and to find ways to help patients adaptively handle their experiences and find ways to reconcile the traumatic event in a healthy way so their brain can deal with it and categorize it appropriately."

The lecturer then described some of the symptoms of PTSD: ongoing high anxiety, irritability, unfounded anger, rapid heart rate, sweating, tightness in chest, a feeling of being trapped or unable to move, recurring nightmares, and an inability to experience positive emotions such as happiness or joy.

The lecturer continued "Now if you remember your first-year psychology class, you may remember your lecturer informing you that if you were over twenty-five, your brain was now stable and there would be no more growth; the only changes after about age twenty-five would be the brain going downhill. But we now know that PTSD changes your brain significantly, but in a maladaptive way. Thus, if we can see a rapid change in how the brain is organized because of a traumatic event, it suggests that the brain can be altered by even a limited event. Whereas long-term brain changes are often structural in nature, there can also be procedural brain changes. Think of learning a new skill, for example playing the piano. You learn some notes the first day, but when you return the next day, you don't automatically start where you left off. You go back a bit before going forward. It takes practice to gain a skill". I thought ah yes that makes sense.

The lecturer then suggested that "Traumatic events affect one's biochemistry and result in associative memories, often bad. We do not want these to become structural or procedural memories that are strengthened and respond to in a maladaptive way; we don't want to practice them. We want to rewire how the patient responds to these symptoms so they can handle and categorize them.

Researchers are using a number of ways to alter unwanted memories and stop them from reoccurring and entering a long-term state. The primary focus is on how to train the brain to handle these intrusive memories, which is essential for dealing with trauma. How do patients reconcile what has happened to them and how do they regain control? A number of studies are underway by the hospital and our university affiliates on that topic."

The lecturer described some of the approaches they were trying. Some involved using MRI to observe the brain while the patient was listening to an account of their trauma, and then working on ways to change the activity seen in the brain. The first and most fundamental strategy seemed to be trying to replace the negative emotional response or typical triggers with more appropriate responses. The speaker described one method that involved having the patient write out their story in great detail, including what they were feeling, smelling, and hearing during the event. Week after week they would read their stories over again, breaking down the details, dealing with the event, and discussing their emotions. The goal was to dull the emotional connection to the event and increase separation from it. Doctors can also integrate biofeedback: patients read their stories with the goal of keeping their heart rate, skin temperature, blood pressure—even electroencephalography feedback—stable. The lecturer explained, "If they can train their behavioral output it will influence physiological changes and subsequently neurological changes."

The lecturer showed some "before-and-after" slides of brainwave and biofeedback graphs of patients with PTSD. For the most part the explanations were over my head but I could certainly get the point, which was that the retraining program was working and that some individuals were not only able to handle PTSD better but they were changing their brains in the process. I could understand that the percent changes in symptoms and reductions in stress responses in the patients were remarkable.

Meanwhile, I was becoming a firm believer in neuroscience, even in the idea that everything is brain-based and everyone has the ability to change their brains. This lecture certainly inspired me because I had just experienced a traumatic brain event myself and I certainly wanted to get my brain better.

The presentation included some moving video testimonials in which patients explained how they had gone from living with daily fear and sleepless nights to returning to a normal schedule, some in a matter of weeks (though these were best-case scenarios I was betting). I thought it was phenomenal, and again I wondered, do people know what's going on here, that it's the cutting edge of research? Do people understand the success they're having here?

I realized I needed to do something. I wasn't sure what, but when I got out of this hospital, I was going to make a difference. Things were going to be different.

I was beginning to feel tired again. So much information every day—I wondered how the students at the hospital were able to keep up. I'd had about all I could handle that morning, so I quietly snuck out of the lecture hall, being careful, while closing the door, that not even a click would be heard. As I focused on doing this, someone else popped out the door at the other end of the hall without a thought to the noise—*bash*, as the door closed—and down the hall they went. So much for that.

As I turned down the hall I couldn't help but wonder, again, whether the public had any idea about half of the information that's presented daily in this hospital. It was phenomenal; there was so much to learn. Then I wondered if I should be taking it a bit easier. Maybe I should have gone for coffee with Thomas and Ella; that might have been a little more relaxing. But how could I pass up such an informative lecture? That made me wonder if I might become one of those people who sits in on university lectures for fun. But eating wings and watching hockey or baseball was fun too. So many things I could do. And I knew I was going to have some time off work. I might even retire, which would give me a lot more time. So I'd better think of something productive to do with that time.

I figured I'd have a little fun before I got back to my room to talk with Dr. White so I dropped into the games room. As I walked in, I saw that the research assistants were hard at work with a couple of patients. I assumed this was the morning training session and that after they were finished they would connect with Thomas and me.

I was in luck; the arcade games were not in use. I stepped up to the Pac-Man console, pushed the button, and felt like a kid again. I dodged ghosts, ate some pellets, and on occasion ate some ghosts and fruit. I idly wondered whether the fruit had been placed in the game to encourage kids to eat better. After about twenty minutes I headed to my room. I did not want to miss Dr. White's visit. I wanted out of here. I wanted to get home to my bed and my most comfortable chair. As I moved down the hall, I realized my leg was feeling much better and that my gait (a new word I learned in therapy, meaning how I walk) seemed fairly normal. I mean, I hadn't really thought about it, so it must be pretty much normal. As I got up to the nursing station, I just waved because I could see both nurses were on the phone. They smiled and waved back. I motioned that I would be in my room and Caroline gave me a thumbs up.

Thomas and Ella had not returned yet, but I was sure they would not be far behind me. I gave Leia a quick call to see if she would be able to pick me up this afternoon. I thought I might just take a cab but I knew Leia would have my ass if I didn't call her for a ride. I found my phone and keyed in her number but it went straight to voicemail. I left her a brief message letting her know I would be leaving this afternoon and if she was free about 3:00 I should be ready to go. I guessed she was in class, which was usually the only time she turned her phone off; otherwise, she was glued to it. She had lots of time to get back to me and if she didn't I had a great excuse to just grab a cab or an Uber and head home.

I noticed the room was quieter than usual. I glanced at my roommate and saw that his ventilator had been removed.

***

Downstairs in the coffee shop, Thomas and Ella were just finishing their morning coffee when Thomas remarked, "I wonder if that doctor will be by today. I've been waiting this whole time to see if he would show up."

"Thomas, really. You're bad. That's just not nice. That poor doctor is probably a really busy man and getting entertainment from his, um, struggles—it's not polite."

"Ella darling, I'm in the hospital. You have to allow me a little fun. I had a stroke, you know." Thomas turned slightly in his chair and hung his head, feigning sadness.

Ella rolled her eyes. At this moment she knew Thomas was going to be okay, really okay. She turned back to the article she was reading and lifted her newspaper just high enough to hide her smile.

Ella was reading about research showing how social support networks affect your mental health, especially your level of happiness. The researchers' goal was to use a questionnaire disguised as a metric for free-time activities, so the participants were unaware that the true goal was to discover their overall happiness and how that correlated to what they did in their free time. What Ella found most interesting was that it appeared that people whose free-time activities involved a social component reported more overall happiness with their free time than people who engaged in solo activities.

The study also suggested that there were age-related differences: teens and older people showed high rates of happiness because these age groups had greater social components than participants in their middle years. Ella thought she better make sure she and Thomas remained social, because she also knew that happiness aided in physical recovery. She wanted to keep Thomas happy, social, and active. She didn't think that seemed too much of a tall order since that was pretty much what they did every day anyway. Ella felt even better about their future.

Thomas finished his coffee and looked at his watch. "We should be heading back soon. We can't wait any longer for Doctor Nervous to come by."

"Yes, we should get back." She ignored his second comment. As they walked back Ella said, "We should think about taking a trip when you're feeling better." She wanted to plan something together and maybe go somewhere or see something they hadn't experienced before. "Maybe a cruise would be nice. They make lots of stops and you can see lots of places."

Thomas immediately rejected that idea. "You want to get food poisoning, or be trapped in a tin can with hundreds of people with the flu? And I don't want to be stuck, I want to be able to move around freely in the world at large." He made an expansive gesture.

"There's no curfew onboard and your door is not locked at night, so you can move around the ship as freely as you want."

"Hmph. But you're right, we should plan a vacation. I was thinking of something with a bit more excitement, such as helicopter rides, jet boat tours, or treetop zip lining."

Ella just rolled her eyes. Oh boy; he was going to take advantage of this hospital stay as a bargaining chip and that's going to be tough to argue against, the sly so-and-so.

***

Thomas and Ella reached our room just as Dr. White was coming down the hall. Before they entered I heard Dr. White ask if they wanted to chat in the lounge to give the other patients privacy. I heard Thomas reply, "Okay," which meant I would have to wait a bit longer before I could talk to Dr. White.

I wondered if I had time to go downstairs to grab some food to supplement my breakfast, but decided I didn't. I did notice my large roommate was severed a meal yet had not eaten it, since he had never been awake. Hmm... I thought I would take a look and as I started to make my way over to see what I could grab my phone rang and I nearly jumped through the roof. It was Leia. "Leia. I know I'm in the hospital and though it's a good place for a heart attack, I would rather not have one!" though of course she had no idea what I was taking about.

"Huh?"

"Never mind. I... was just resting. Were you in class?"

Leia answered with an exasperated tone. "Yes Dad. Otherwise I would have had my phone on."

"No worries, honey. I'm just about to see Dr. White, and I expect I'll be out of here this afternoon. I have a training session and then I should be good to go. Can, or do you want to, pick me up?"

"Of course! What time should I be there?"

"I expect about 2:30-ish should be good. If I'm not ready you can find me in the training lab."

"Okay, sounds good. I'll see you then," she said happily. "Love you, Dad."

I smiled. "Love you too, kid; see you soon." I lay back against the crisp white pillow. It was comfortable but it made a crinkling sound every time I moved my head. I couldn't wait to be able to move my head without hearing that sound.

As I lay there waiting for Dr. White, I was still a little apprehensive about the news she may deliver. I felt fine and I was ready to go home but I knew of people who had felt fine and then a physician had given them weeks to live. I wished she had come in and spoken with me first; I hate waiting around, though truly, where did I have to go?

This certainly had not been a great week in my life, but I hoped things would get a lot better from here. I stared out the window looking at what a gray day it was again today, kind of like my mood. In that moment I longed for some sunshine and maybe an open road and a fast car. While I was at it, maybe having my youth back for one more day would be good too. I wanted just one more of those days when responsibility was just a word, a day topped off with a few beers at a pub with friends, the jukebox playing our favorite songs. Maybe I'd catch the eye of a pretty lady, and if I was lucky I would take her home. Those times were as close to heaven on Earth as I could get. The thought brought out a loud sigh, and I was grateful there was no one around but my comatose roommate.

Just as I regained my composure Dr. White came into my room with great speed, but I had the feeling she did most things with speed. She sat down on the bed next to me and asked how I was feeling.

"Fine—and ready to go."

"I understand that you're ready. Please know that my goal is to get everyone up and moving along as soon as possible, but when someone has had treatment and recanalization of occluded areas of the brain, we need to monitor them and ensure the treatment has been effective and everything is working as it should. We can't be too hasty.

"When you had your stroke, you got to the hospital quickly, which is great, but we often see the height of damage at around twenty-four to thirty-six hour mark, thus the need to rescan and keep you in the hospital under observation. However, I can also tell you that quick intravenous thrombolysis treatment like you received can help minimize damage through reperfusion of affected areas. And you got it pretty quickly." I was getting antsy, waiting for her to tell me if I was going home or not.

"Things we typically watch for during this period are failed reperfusion, which can result in severe swelling, which often goes beyond our ability to treat without an invasive procedure to relieve the pressure, which would mean a longer recovery, to say the least.[28] But in your case I did not see any issues—the swelling and damage are subsiding as I expected. Because your blockage was relatively brief, I don't expect to see any long-term deficits. Hopefully you can regain a hundred percent, or at least ninety-five percent, of function, which in your case may still be better than the average person," she smiled at that point, which reminded me she really cared.

Dr. White paused before continuing. "However, I am aware of your visual field deficit, which is of concern to me. I'm hoping that in a month, or maybe as long as three months, it will improve, especially with the early training we've put in place. Dr. Stern will also concentrate on retraining your visual field in hopes of bringing it back to normal. We might need to take your license but I will assess your visual field at your next appointment. If you still have 120 degrees you're good to go, but in the meantime, please do not drive or I will report it and you know what a pain it can be to get your license back."

Wow, she was serious. She wants to take my license! Is she crazy? I could drive better with an eye and half than most people on the road. This was absolutely ridiculous. But I played it cool and didn't say anything. I would figure it out.

"You're scheduled for training right after lunch. After that I will have your paperwork ready and you will be discharged. That said, I wouldn't mind keeping you an extra day, if you want to stay."

I shook my head firmly. "No."

"I didn't think so but it was worth a try. Anyway, you're scheduled for ongoing training for three days a week, and I will coordinate your first appointment with your first training day back, which will be a week from today. We'll also do another scan that day, so you should plan to be here for a while that day. If you have any concerns you can contact my office directly—numbers will be on your discharge paperwork, along with your prescriptions and post-discharge instructions. Also, Dr. Stern will want to access to your medical file to measure progress and I would like to be able to review your training progress, so there will be consent forms in your package for you to sign if you're okay with us sharing information. Note that only we will have access to this information and it will not be shared outside your treatment circle.

"Finally, just for your peace of mind, when Dr. Stern presents her research, she never presents results for individual subjects, she presents data in group form, so no one would be able to recognize medical or training information." She gave me a moment to take that all in. "Do you have any questions?"

"I'm just wondering... you suggest I keep active and exercise moderately, but I was hoping to quantify just what moderate is to you. To me it would be a few weights here and there and a three-mile run, maybe with some walking; things such as that."

Dr. White smiled, "I think maybe just keep it to some walking for the next couple of weeks. After that, if you want to run slowly, build up to it and listen to your body, not your desires, Detective. Keep it low key for a bit. I will be checking in with you regularly and we can sort it out and see how things are going as you progress."

I was going to ask about sex but I figured I would read through all the instructions and maybe check online instead, and perhaps bring that up at my next visit if need be. It wasn't like this was going to be a concern anytime soon. But you never know. I figured I should be prepared anyway. "Okay, sounds good. Dr. White, thank you for all your care, and your time. I appreciate it. I'll see you soon."

She smiled. "You are very welcome. You take it easy, and I will see you shortly." And with that she was off, with her long white coat trailing after her.

Moments later Thomas and Ella came back into the room. Knowing I was speaking with Dr. White, they'd given me some time. "How was coffee?"

Thomas replied, "Splendid despite the setting, and the coffee was actually much better than one would expect in a hospital." He paused. "So? Are they springing you today, Detective?"

I laughed. "Yes they are. Thank heavens. I think I might have left anyway, so I'm glad we're parting on good terms. How about you, Thomas? Is today your lucky day?"

Ella answered. "Dr. White said she would release him to my care if he promised to be a good boy and do what he was told."

"And did he promise?"

"Yes, he did, and I'm going to hold him to it."

"You'd best be on good behavior then, Thomas."

Thomas chuckled and replied, "I guess, but what is life without adding a little mischievous adventure now and then?" He sent a sly smile in Ella's direction. She shook her fist at him.

What a couple. I was very happy for Thomas and he looked as if he was doing well. I certainly wanted to keep in touch with them once we'd left the hospital. "Say, how's about we trade numbers? You never know when you're going to need to talk to a guy who's had a stroke." I pulled out my phone, ready to add them.

Ella got out her phone. "Absolutely!" We exchanged numbers.

Lunch came and went and that's all that needs to be said about that. My training assistant, Erin, was exceptionally cheery today during our session, which made me wonder if they were losing participants and had been ordered to be super-excited in hopes of retaining them. I did notice today that I seemed to be much better at the virtual tasks, even just a day after my first try. They really must be on to something here. I said as much to Erin.

"Absolutely. I totally agree with the researchers here. It only makes sense to train what was injured, right? If it was your leg, we would help you walk and strengthen it to get back to good functional use, and the physiotherapist would insist on training regularly. So, since your brain was injured it makes sense to train your brain and strengthen it."

It was so logical it made me wonder again why this was not standard practice. Of course, I understood the financial and logistical complications, but something needed to be done; someone needed to do something.

suddenly realized the only question left was whether I was going to be that someone. Was there something I could do to help this cause? Was this a fight I wanted to take up?

These were serious questions. If I was going to take on the fight, I was going to need serious resolve, never mind resources and an understanding of what could be done and how one gets things done. That question in and of itself was surely going to take time to figure out, and I was not sure I *could* figure it out, especially not on my own.

Leia arrived to pick me up. The drive home was surreal for me. I remembered quite clearly bringing Leia home from the hospital after she was born and now, she was driving me home from the hospital. She was very upbeat because I think she wanted to keep things positive and make sure I was comfortable, so she was talking a lot; I think she was nervous. That also reminded me of bringing her home as a newborn. Just as I had been, she seemed unsure of what was next. In fact, I remembered actually saying to my wife, "What do we do now?" Funny how things evolve. I did my best to reassure Leia and let her know I was quite alright. And then I stared out the window, wondering, what next?

So many thoughts come flooding back when you're in a transition in your life. I thought that after my stay in the hospital I would be done taking stock and reflecting, but apparently my brain was not. I think what I was lamenting most was not having a special someone in my life. When you're young, you take so many people, and things in general, for granted and you don't take time to enjoy the little things, like a perfect warm afternoon when the sun just keeps shining, not a cloud in the sky, a soft breeze in the air, t-shirt and shorts are dress of the day. How many days like that had I ignored? Or the nights on the town with a wonderful woman who stares at you all night, her eyes burning just for you, engaging you and challenging you with insightful thoughts and feelings, an intellect to match her beauty. Oh, the things I have missed.

I did remember, during our drive, that I wanted to get a dog and I thought it would be great to take Leia along to look at some prospects, though I didn't want to do too much looking. I hadn't thought about what kind of dog to get. Maybe a husky or a golden retriever.

The car ride was becoming a little hypnotic, with the joints in the highway bumping one after the other. The day was still gray and it looked as if it was about to rain again. I noticed that the grass at the side of the road was turning brown; summer was ending. It was uninspiring. The radio was on, but not too loud because I knew Leia wanted to keep the conversation going. A Kenny Chesney song was playing that reminded me of the beach, which made me think a trip to the ocean would be excellent. But then what would I do with the dog I was going to get? Maybe Leia would watch it for me.

I turned to Leia. "Would you mind watching my dog for me if I had one and if I went on a trip?"

Leia laughed out loud. "For most people I would say that's a pretty random question, but for you, Dad, well, I know your thinking. So I will simply say yes, I would watch your dog for you if you had one and you went on a trip. Now may I ask, are you getting a dog, and are you going on a trip?"

"I have no firm plans yet. I need to complete my training before I do anything. But I thought it might be nice to get a dog, and I thought maybe a trip to the beach to get away from this gray weather would be a nice change too."

Leia asked quietly, "But what about work, Dad?"

I sighed and said, "I'm assuming I'll have a lot of time off. I have about a thousand sick days and holidays saved up, so I'm guessing I'll use a few of those up and then maybe retire after that."

"Wow! You want to retire? Really?"

"Maybe from the police force anyway. But you know me; I won't retire from life. I have quite a few things in mind and I could use the time."

Leia nodded. "That makes sense. I find it hard to imagine you sitting in a chair all day long playing chess online."

I laughed out loud at the thought of sitting around all day. Not a chance. No. I had some things I wanted to do and they certainly involved my to-do list. But first things first. Where would I find a dog?

CHAPTER 14
PASSAGES

That evening Bruce Grafton passed away in the Stroke Center. Dr. Pattern heard from the staff that his daughter and ex-wife had come in the morning before Bruce had passed, so they got to say their goodbyes and were able to make arrangements to get Bruce's body home.

Dr. Pattern thought how ironic it was that there were so many decisions to be made when a loved one died, which of course was the worst time to make decisions and to do the necessary paperwork. But the need arose often because so many people resisted making their final arrangements. Understanding one's mortality was hard enough, never mind figuring out which songs you wanted played at your funeral or the type of flowers you should have.

Eli found that many physicians had a good sense of their own mortality and had either made arrangements or given explicit instructions to loved ones on what they would like done, which was usually very minimal. But most people figured, why on earth would you want to spend any time planning your own funeral? Boy, that sounds like a lot of fun. Maybe that would be a good conversation topic for his first date with the blue-lipstick barista, if he ever managed to ask her out. Maybe it would be a good icebreaker conversation! Or maybe, he thought, ideas like that were why he was still single.

When he finished the day's paperwork, Dr. Pattern headed to the coffee shop. Today was going to be the day he would ask that girl out.

On Saturday, Casey and Cassandra were on the plane heading back home. Casey was resting on the seat next to Cassandra; amazingly, it had been empty. When the flight attendant came by, Cassandra ordered two drinks, "One for her and one for me." The flight attendant gave Cassandra an odd look as Cassandra opened both trays. Once the attendant had moved down the aisle, Cassandra clinked the two plastic glasses together and then drank them both down in quick succession. She touched the urn on the seat beside her. "That one was for you, sis."

Cassandra thought how just days ago, she had talked to Casey on the phone about plans for moving out, trying to get Casey's thoughts on what she should do. She had relied on Casey so much—her sister and best friend. She couldn't imagine Casey not being there on the other end of the phone, or a quick text away. She couldn't grasp the idea of never again receiving a silly photo of Casey doing something crazy somewhere in world.

The entire hospital experience was so draining, and Cassandra had had so little sleep, but still she had to make such important decisions, decisions she would normally call Casey about. Casey was the one who could make those types of decisions fearlessly. Cassandra kept going over it all in her head. Had she done the right thing?

Casey's treatment had been aggressive, and complications can arise. The complication for Casey had been an ischemic blockage elsewhere in her brain. In addition, in the early stage of her treatment, maintaining the balance of pressure within the brain and body had been a delicate thing; complications can and do happen. Cassandra had been informed of what was happening to Casey at the time, and she was given an estimate of around 70% likelihood of a lifelong deficit related to the treatment, and that was the best estimate.

Dr. Montoya noted that based on what he knew about her current brain state, Casey would not return to her normal self and would need lifelong care at some level (what level he would or could not say), if she recovered at all. But Dr. Montoya had explained that they would do their best and continue to help Casey as long as Cassandra wished them to. Cassandra had come to realize that what that conversation was truly about was choosing whether her sister would live or die, right now. That was an impossible situation. She had just arrived at the hospital and had barely been able to comprehend the situation as it was, and now they expected her to determine whether her sister lived in a reduced state, if that was even possible, or whether she should ask them to stop what they are doing and let Casey die.

That was not right, Cassandra thought. Why had she been forced into that position? She was angry at Casey. Why had Casey put her in such a position? Which, of course, was ridiculous, because Cassandra knew that was the last thing Casey would do. But she could not rationalize any of it. Casey was all she had left. What would she do on her own? She had no family left to help her raise her kids, since she knew her marriage was done. What was she going to do?

She remembered being in the hospital staring out the large waiting room window facing the city, which offered a view of people going about their day, none of them aware of the decisions she was being asked to make at that moment. Cassandra's thoughts were feverish. Her head was spinning. She wanted to be selfish, to tell them to fix her or at least try. She wanted to take Casey home with her no matter what. She wanted her just to be there with her, even if it was only a part of her. She needed Casey.

As Cassandra had turned to Dr. Montoya to tell him this, she had begun to cry uncontrollably, the tears streaming down her face so that her shirt began to stain like she had just come in out of the rain. As she began to speak, to tell him to save her, save her now, all she could whisper was, "Thank you, doctor, for all you have done for Casey, but... it's okay to let her go."

Dr. Montoya had put some forms in front of her to sign. As she reached for the pen she could see her hands were limp and tired, and her heart ached, but she signed them, and that was that. She felt she had signed Casey's life away with the stroke of a pen.

Though Cassandra was surprised by the words that actually came out of her mouth, she knew it was the right thing to do. She knew she had to let her go and if she didn't, she would regret whatever state Casey remained in. And from what Cassandra had been able to discern from the nurses and physicians, that was most likely not going to be anything Casey would find tolerable. So, in the end, the decision should not have been that difficult because Casey had been a carefree soul and Cassandra knew that trapping her anywhere, especially inside her own body, her worst fear, would have been the most selfish act of her life. She could not bear the idea of seeing Casey that way, instead of out doing what she loved, and for Casey, that meant whatever she fancied that day. But none of that made it easy.

In the days that followed, Cassandra got Casey's affairs in order as best she could before she left the city. The worst part was packing up Casey's apartment. It was so unsettling to have to pack her everyday items knowing she would never use them again. It was still impossible for Cassandra to believe she was really gone. The only way she could manage to get through it was to imagine that Casey was moving home and Cassandra was helping her pack. She decided not to purge very much because she didn't know what was or was not important, plus she didn't have a lot of time; she needed to get back home to the kids.

She made no attempt to speak to anyone that knew Casey. She had no desire to inform anyone of her sister's death, other than her employer, since she still couldn't accept it herself, and she really didn't know how to get in contact with Casey's friends. She did speak with the landlord, which tied up the most important loose ends. He was able to purchase Casey's furniture, which solved the issue of moving those items, and the extra money was useful for the cost of moving the remainder of Casey's stuff home. As for bills and other miscellaneous things, she could not even imagine what to do right now. They would have to wait.

As Cassandra sat on the plane drinking with Casey, she couldn't help going over her memories of her sister. She still had lots of photos on her phone that Casey had sent, even as recently as a week ago. What was funny was that she had been at the zoo a couple of weeks ago and she had sent Cassandra a selfie with a tiger in the background. Casey reminded Cassandra of a tiger at a zoo when she was stuck somewhere she didn't want to be: she just wanted to *go*; you could see it in her eyes. Like in her teen years, Cassandra thought. To imprison Casey anywhere for any length of time would bring out that look in her eye, the sad tiger at the zoo look, longing to run. Cassandra thought, well sis, you are truly free now, out in the universe. Go wherever you desire. Cassandra knew that Casey believed our energy never died, it merely transformed. Casey told her once, maybe after a night of drinking, that life is a collection of circumstances. They can be ordinary or extraordinary; the choice is yours.

Those words had stuck with Cassandra through the years, perhaps because it was so early in the morning when Casey had called that time, or maybe because it was such a profound and lucid thing for Casey to say. It's funny the things you remember about people after they're gone. Like when Casey was a little girl she would lie on her bed on a lazy late afternoon when the sun would hit their room just right, and she would hold up a crystal in the sunlight and let the colours unfold like a rainbow on the white bedroom wall. Their parents believed that neutral colours were best in the house in case they moved, so Casey took it upon herself to add colour. Casey did the things Cassandra dared not. She was carefree and everything else Cassandra knew she could never be. She was the rainbow of colour in Cassandra's life and Cassandra was certain now that not a day would go by when she would not think of Casey.

Chapter 15
A New Journey

There was a knock at my door. I was in the middle of a mid-morning nap after having breakfast with Leia before she headed out for the day. I wondered who it could be.

As I headed to the door, I heard a familiar voice. "Declan, I know you had a stroke but seriously how slow are you?" It was Abigail. She knocked again.

I shouted, "Good lord, give me a second; you are so impatient."

I unlocked the door to see Abigail, smiling, holding two cups of coffee. "About time, these are hot."

"Geez, I take a few days off and you're the boss now."

Abigail smiled. "Well someone needs to get the work done and we have cases on the go, remember? And now there's only me and if you've forgotten, I'm still new at this and I could use some help."

"Oh I know you could use the help; I've seen you in action," I said, adding a fake chuckle.

It was so nice to see Abigail and she seemed very concerned about me. I know she would have made her way to the hospital, but she made it clear she wanted to give me space and did not know if I would have family there are not. We had a long talk and I brought her up to speed on pretty much everything that was going on with me. I told her I truly felt like I was going to be okay. I talked to her about my stroke and the training program, and about my hospital experience. I described the current state of affairs with stroke patients in general.

She gave me an update on our current cases, and I asked her to email me updates regularly so I could respond with thoughts on directions we should take as we investigated. Then I finally got to the harder conversation, letting her know that I would be taking a bunch of sick days and then some holidays as well. I did not have the heart to tell her yet that I would not be going back to work at all. I wanted to sort of leave that door open for now, in case.

It was a great visit and I knew she would be just fine without me. I was hoping to help her much more but I told her I would do my best and keep in regular contact with her. I made sure she had me on speed dial and I told her no matter the time of day, she could give me a call and I would give her some direction or advice.

When she left, she gave me an uncharacteristic hug, as if she knew, maybe, I would not be back. After all, she was a smart cookie. That's why I had brought her on board.

The rest of my day consisted of lounging in my chair and working on my in-home exercises. After that I spent some time finding a new recipe for dinner. I thought I would get dinner ready before Leia got back so she didn't need to do it after a busy day. I decided on a ham and asparagus frittata. It looked pretty good in the picture so I walked down to the corner grocery, got the stuff, and gave it a shot. I figured if I made it big enough, we could have leftovers the next day; after all, tomorrow was a training day for me and I figured I would be at the hospital most of the day.

After it was prepared, I popped it in the oven and sat down to look online for shelters that had dogs needing homes. I wondered if puppies would be hard to find.

As I looked through one of many dog rescue websites, I thought, wow, it's just like a dating site: the more attractive the dog, the greater its advantage, in this case the more likely it is to get rescued.

None of them seemed to fit my exact requirements, though, and there were certainly no purebreds on this list. But the more I looked, the less that mattered. I kept scanning the pages, and I could see I was nearing the end, and then I spotted a dog by the name of Abigale. That was funny, I thought, and maybe also a sign.

Abigale's profile noted she was a shepherd mix, six months old and weighing twenty-eight pounds. She had the cutest face. Her picture reminded me a bit of the dog, Max, from *How the Grinch Stole Christmas*, but she was darker on her back. I originally thought I would have a much bigger dog but when I thought about it more, a medium-sized dog would be nice to cuddle up with at night to watch TV. Plus Leia agreed to watch her when I was away and I thought she would not have as much trouble with a smaller dog. My mind was set!

Okay, now how did I get this dog? Was there a complicated process involved, where the agency checks your background, references, and so on? There usually is, which always struck me as ironic, because we let anyone have a child. And we, the police, spend significant amounts of time mopping up family incidents that involve those not so great parents. And when things get bad, they really get bad. I hated attending child apprehensions—or worse, tragic events in a family home.

I forced my focus to return to my dog-to-be. I dug further. Apparently, to adopt one of the shelter's dogs I needed to be of legal age—okay, check; have some ID—check; have money and time to look after the dog, and finally, I would have to spend an hour with an adoption counselor discussing the responsibilities of having a pet; check, check, and check, I guess. I got on the phone and gave the place a call. I told them which dog I was interested in and I suggested that maybe I could do most of the preliminary stuff over the phone so picking up the dog would be quick since I had recently been in the hospital and spending long periods away from home is difficult (I lied), but I wanted to make sure I could "reserve" this dog. Surprisingly, they agreed. I would pick the dog up the day after tomorrow. I was excited to tell Leia the news when she got home. Tonight we would go out and get all the dog stuff: a bed, toys, food, the lot.

Dinner would be ready soon and I expected Leia home soon as well. I had completed my home training for the day and this left me a little time... to do what? I had rested all morning; I had given my word that I would hold off working out, but I might get in a bit of a walk tonight after dinner. Maybe Leia would join me if she didn't have any pressing homework. In the meantime I looked at my to-do list: I could either start working on my will or I could work on my idea to help those who could not help themselves. That made me think back to the lectures I had listened in on at the hospital and about the program I was so fortunate to be involved in. I was definitely going to do something to promote it.

I drafted a basic mission statement for a non-profit foundation I'd decided to start—right now. No time like the present. I started working out the details, talking aloud to myself. The statement would have to involve providing access to information and resources wherever and whenever possible for people who wanted the help and had a desire to improve their physical or cognitive function after a stroke.

Maybe that was all it needed to be: The Stroke Support Foundation would provide free access to information and training for individuals who wanted and needed support services after experiencing a stroke or stroke-related event. It was as simple as that. That would be the working mission statement for the organization until I got something more formal in place.

So now what? How could I make a difference? There were a ton of different stroke information sites online; why and how were people not getting the information? Or why were they not accessing the information? Maybe the information was too dense. Maybe more concise statements that could be automatically sent to the individual would be more effective, to get them thinking and wanting to learn more, kind of like news headlines or alert texts sent to your phone telling you it's time to get active or asking if you've completed your homework.

But there was no point in sending information unless individuals have a way to access it. So everyone was going to need a device, like the tablets Thomas and I had been given. Most people had a smartphone or tablet, so just adding an app or program would work for them. But if I could get tablets to people who needed them through the foundation, we could preload them with all the elements that were on mine.

In addition, access to the hospital's lectures—on any topic, not just stroke-related topics, should be an option. The stroke-related lectures would be very helpful. I could work with the hospital to set up remote access to the lectures, but we could start by preloading the individuals' devices with lectures related to stroke recovery. Having information already on the device would help people in remote areas where internet access was unreliable, and individuals could watch the lectures whenever they wanted.

I was getting excited now. A blog would also be a great idea, and essential to providing ongoing communication to participants. It would also be a place for patients and families to ask questions and receive support from other participants. People can do their own research on the web, but they could end up reading information that's not verified or vetted. There's a lot of misinformation out there and that's something we would need to ensure did not end up on our site. I would have to monitor posts to ensure people were not offering medical opinions and were only describing their personal experiences and maybe what worked for them and what didn't. Visits to the doctor after a stroke must create a lot of questions and concerns about an individual's progress or lack thereof. A page of answers to common questions and concerns would be very helpful.

A professional site would be an excellent addition as well. Researchers and clinicians could log in and access research articles and resources to use with their participants at their own hospitals. I could list common funding strategies as well it could help researchers find funding, though I currently had no idea where or how such funding was found.

But I would figure that out. I would figure it all out. I knew all the ideas I was coming up with were best-case scenarios, and I realized I currently had no idea how to get it all done. But I always found a way. For now, I would dream what I wanted to see and then start on the logistics later. I would get some Bristol board and start mapping out all these ideas so I could see all the information at once.

If I started this organization, I would need a lot of funding myself to get tablets and to have a website and blog built. Oh boy; this was all sounding very exhausting suddenly, and I had only been working on the idea for a few minutes. Where would I find funding? I figured government organizations and stroke care organizations would be a no brainer. I'm no expert but it seemed like such a program would reduce healthcare costs so they should be interested.

There were so many small details I would need to work out. I realized I would need an entire team to help me with this endeavor. I would certainly need to get the hospital on board, which would include getting Dr. Stern interested in helping with contacts and speaking with the hospital about getting access to the information via permissions to load lectures and so on.

I wondered if Thomas and Ella might be interested in helping. I thought they would be excellent resources and I was sure they could lend some insight.

I resolved to talk the whole thing out a bit with Leia tonight and see what she thought.

When Leia got home, she sniffed the air. "Yum! You made dinner, Dad? It smells great."

"Thanks, kid. I thought it would be a nice treat. Even though I know you're in take-care-of-Dad mode, since you're staying here for a while I thought I might spend some time taking care of you too."

She gave me a big hug. "I'm glad you're feeling well, Dad." She paused and looked at me. "I'm not ready to lose you. I still need you."

That made me feel so good. It was nice to still be needed. Leia set the table and we sat down to eat. First, I asked her how school was going, and she talked about all the reading that was required. "I'm taking a half course and the professor expects us to write two papers, two exams, weekly assignments, and an independent study paper! It's the work of a full-year course. I'm thinking of dropping it."

"It's important to manage your time in your undergraduate years, and if dropping a course is really what makes sense, then you should feel good about your decision and drop it. And then plan how you will make up the course later. When I was in school, I would map out each week, with the times I was going to study, and I would allot time for writing papers and reading, and I would plan my free time as well. I always looked ahead and I'd build in buffer days here and there just in case I got behind in anything. I know it's tough, but it's not far off from what you'll need to do when you get out in the 'real world.'"

Leia sighed heavily. "But it's not like when you went to school. Things are so condensed now and everything moves quickly. Sometimes I feel there's an inequity between me and some of the other students. When things get tough it's hard not to think of students that get extra time with no consequences." I was puzzled. Leia explained, "Some students have 'accommodations.'" Before I could ask, she said, "There are a lot of students with accommodations of some sort, people who have identified learning issues, and so for example they get extra time to write exams, extra time on assignments, or other things, like laptops or whatever."

I frowned. "When they get their degree, does it note they completed it with accommodations, cause if they needed help then wouldn't it be fair to note that?"

"Nope, it doesn't."

"Wow. But wouldn't that seem fair? Since they're not completing the work the same way as everyone else, if they get hired somewhere that would be important for an employer to know, wouldn't it?"

"I don't know, Dad. I guess their employers find out the hard way. It would be tough, though, if it was your first day at NASA and they needed some quick calculations."

I chuckled. "I guess that would be a difficult day for a lot of people." I didn't really want to get into a big discussion about what was wrong with our current education system, which I think would have lasted all night. I wanted to talk to Leia about my plans.

So as I was getting out some ice cream for dessert— chocolate, of course—I started to explain my upcoming plans. I would start with the fact that I was getting a dog, and planned to move on to the organization I was about to start.

I brought our bowls to the table. "So, Leia. I think it's time to add a new member to our family." I had a fun plan to draw her into a conversation in which she would have to guess what that meant, with me taking my time, being vague, not explaining.

Straight off she answered, "Oh, you found a dog you want?"

I had forgotten that I had talked to her two days before about maybe getting a dog.

Deflated, I replied, "Yes, good guess." She had ruined my fun. "I found it online at a local shelter. She needs to be rescued."

"Awesome! Dad, that is so great to rescue a dog. What kind is it? What's its name?"

I filled her in. "Her name is Abigale and she's a shepherd mix."

"Is that a police thing?"

I laughed and shrugged. "Do you think we could pop out tonight and get all the dog stuff we're going to need from the pet store at the plaza? I would drive but of course I promised I wouldn't for a while."

"Of course!" We ate our ice cream, and I think we were both excited to go to the pet store and see what they had. Somehow I had not gotten around to talking about my organization-to-be. But I could get to that later.

The pet mega-store looked like Wal-Mart for animals. I was amazed at how much stuff there was in this store, though really, I should not have been surprised because I knew people whose pets were their children and they spared no expense. This store had everything you could possibly imagine and more. I saw dog pajamas. Really. Dog pajamas. Why would a dog need pajamas? And why would a dog need a bed—like, an actual bed? But I saw those too.

Leia went straight to the back of the store to look at all the pets for sale. I was able to find the only salesperson over the age of twenty and explained that I was getting a six-month-old shepherd cross tomorrow. "I need the basics. And just so you know, this dog is not a child substitute. We need food, a *dog* bed, not a piece of furniture, and maybe a few things to chew on besides my furniture."

The clerk laughed. "Gotcha." He led me around the store. "Since you've got a puppy coming, especially one from a shelter, it may need to be house trained."

"Oh. Okay." He handed me training pads. He also found us a leash system, puppy food, and a dog bed. "You may need a kennel for him..."

"Her."

"...her, to sleep in at night or when you're out. Crate training is always a good idea."

I figured I could decide later if that was going to be necessary, if Abigale would not stay in her bed or destroyed the house when we were out.

We passed by Leia playing with a pen of kittens. "Traitor," I said with a wink as I walked by.

We picked up some bones for her to chew. "Otherwise," the sales guy noted, "she's going to chew anything she can, because she is a puppy, and puppies chew." By the time we were done, we had a cartload of items, even though I had only wanted the basics. I looked at the pile and realized that's what I had. When the cashier rang it up, I wondered if I was at a pet store or a jewelry store.

When I had paid for everything, I had to go looking for Leia to help me load the car. She had found a very talkative macaw and was having a good chat. She saw me and realized I was done and hurried to give me a hand.

After we loaded the car I asked if she wanted to get a cup of tea and take a walk around the plaza before we headed home. "Or do you have a lot of homework?"

She thought for a moment. "I think I *will* drop that course, so that means I do have a bit of time tonight. Yay," she said quietly.

We picked up tea and walked around the plaza, window shopping and chatting. I thought this would be a great time to bring up my idea for the Stroke Support Foundation. When I first mentioned that name and gave her the very basics of the idea, she laughed and gave me the "really, Dad?" look. But as I continued to explain, she seemed to understand the reason and the motivation behind the idea, and saw that I was truly serious.

But when I talked about providing tablets to patients, she said, "That doesn't sound reasonable. Where would these tablets come from? You would need a ton of money to fund a project like that." She continued to poke holes in the idea. "You would also need some really web-savvy people to set up and run a site for you and to help with tech support and stuff."

"I know…"

"Would you have an interactive program on the site or is it standalone? Would it run through a third-party system, because you might need a programmer as well."

My balloon was being burst.

She continued. "If you have apps that need to run or you want to develop apps for downloading you would need an app developer. So from a tech standpoint, you would really need, like, *significant* help."

I interjected, "It would seem I have my first board advisor. You seem to have the troubleshooting skills and you understand a number of the issues. And so far, these are just ideas. As I said. Ideas."

"Sorry, Dad. But I have friends that work in this field and I know there can be a *lot* of work involved in just the simplest applications sometimes, and that's time I do not have."

"Well, Dr. Stern, who runs the program at the hospital, has a number of these programs already preloaded on my tablet, so that stuff's already developed. I was planning to see if I could partner with her in getting access to information and help with setting up this material. I know I need help."

The night air had a chill and it was starting to rain a little, but we stayed along the covered sidewalk as we strolled. I could see that Leia was trying to work out some of the issues she had brought up. She began, "Well, if you partner with Dr. Stern, she would have access to a lot of the resources you'll need to get set up. But as I said I do have a couple of friends in the computer programming department who are required to complete projects as part of their degree. Maybe they could do some programming or the website set-up at no cost. They could probably also put in place an easy way to keep on top of the site, so you could manage it yourself via a back door into the system." She was coming around. "This actually sounds pretty cool, Dad. I'm proud of you. I hope I make you proud someday."

I smiled. "You already have, honey." She gave me a big smile back and a long hug.

Leia and I talked a bit more as we walked back to the car. We had actually completed a few laps of the strip mall and I felt like I had actually gotten in a good walk. My legs were tired, which I was happy about because I really wanted to get some exercise. Since we had been chatting most of the time, I think Leia had forgotten the whole reason she was staying with me.

When we got home and unloaded all the stuff, Lei headed to her room to do some reading. I sat in comfortable chair and added a few lines to the diary on my tablet. I paused, thinking about which side I was going to post on, private or public? I decided the public side was a great place to lay out my idea for an organization. That way I would be talking directly to the researchers, so they could comb through my ideas, and maybe they would have some time to try to work out some of the logistics before I approached them directly with my requests.

After listening to Dr. Stern and Dr. White, I knew that time was the most sought-after commodity for clinicians and researchers, so I didn't think yet another request on their time would be welcomed overly much, unless things were already sorted out. There are so many worthwhile endeavors that researchers and clinicians must limit what they can do. Maybe a guy with some time on his hands and a great interest in helping people recover from strokes was something they could use.

I spent the next hour or so writing up some basic points about the direction I was planning on taking with my new organization. I was going to try to work through some of the logistics of setting things up, but I came to realize that I didn't know what I didn't know about setting something like this up. So I abandoned the process for now and instead developed some more overarching goals.

I thought maybe to be inspiring I should put forth my aspirations for the organization and let the experts in the field tell me what I needed to do to get there. After all, many of the world's great discoveries have come from individuals daring to reach for the stars. I certainly didn't believe my idea was as monumental as that. So maybe it wouldn't be too difficult to set up.

I spent some time outlining the main features and goals, including the all-import access to information for people who had little help, and the need to bring in as many participants as possible. I added the goal of tracking the program in relation to time on tasks. For instance, could more time on tasks be related to recovery rates? I wasn't sure if that would be a feasible option, but I did think researchers would like to have data of this nature, so it might be a good selling point for them.

I was starting to feel exhausted; it was late. But I did my best to set down my major points. I thought the result would be a good starting point for a discussion with Dr. Stern at our next training session.

After finishing my work on the public side, I wrote a little in my private diary. I was actually really glad this private area existed, because sometimes it's difficult even to talk to family about how you're feeling because you don't want to worry them.

But I was still really concerned about my health. What were the chances I would have another stroke? If I did, could it be worse than the one I just had? Was it normal to have headaches for days after a stroke, or does that mean something is wrong? I had been lucky this time. Would I regain my full functional ability if it happened again? What if I didn't get that portion of my eyesight back? Would I lose my driver's license for good? Not being able to drive anymore would be a significant blow to my independence. Did physicians know how important a license was to a person? How about sleeping? Would I be able to go to sleep? Would I wake up? Was I okay being at home now or should I have stayed in the hospital one more day? I was thinking about all of that and more. But it actually felt good to put it down on "paper."

It was the time of night when your mind really starts to drift. I started thinking about how I could download my consciousness to a hard drive, which I read somewhere was possible. Then maybe my daughter could boot me up on her computer when she was lonely and missed her dad. I laughed out loud and shut off the tablet.

I turned on the radio. Years ago I'd installed surround sound in my bedroom, which is really cool, and I liked cool stuff. I tuned it to public radio, which can sometimes be a problem because I end up listening to learn about whatever topic they're discussing, rather than falling asleep. Last week I'd learned that a black hole can be identified by understanding the gravitational pull it has on the stars around it, so although we can't see it, we know it's there because of the stars' movements around this black part of space. I also learned that a black hole is so dense and its gravitational pull so strong that not even light can escape. How cool was that little fact?

Tonight they were discussing the impact of global warming on the polar icecaps and the consequences for the rising oceans. They were speaking with Inuit elders, who were explaining the changes in their natural world. The stories were phenomenal and it actually helped me drift off to sleep just listening to them talk. Though the consequences they described were drastic, their voices seemed to hold such wisdom and vision, which strangely offered me comfort and helped me let go for the night, and sleep came.

CHAPTER 16
THE STROKE SUPPORT FOUNDATION

The sun was warm on my face. I was on an incredible beach. White sand and the clearest blue-green water I had ever seen stretched out before me. It seemed endless. The water lapped at my feet as I sat in an oversized beach chair. I was leaning to one side with my elbow on the arm of the chair so I could comfortably hold my book. On the other arm rested a fresh, cool beach cocktail. It was so hot and humid that the droplets forming on the outside of the glass were rolling slowly down and dripping at the base of the stem. It was like a travel commercial. I thought, it's true —time does slow down when you're having some great R&R.

I was on vacation with my girlfriend, a swimsuit model, who had just finished a photo shoot farther down the beach. As she approached, I saw that it had been a topless shoot today and she had not bothered to put her top on afterwards. Beside me now, she leaned in and said, "How's it going, handsome?" and kissed me softly on the cheek. Then for some reason she began licking my cheek. Odd. The licking became more aggressive—she started licking my whole face vigorously. I woke up to see Abigale beside my bed, licking my face full force. "Ewww!" Abigale! You ruined the most wonderful dream!" I rubbed her ears. "You're a silly dog."

I could not be mad at her, though. She had been the m wonderful friend I'd had in a while. But many morn she had woken me up to take her for a walk. I didn't though, since she was making sure I exercised. In addition to the morning walks, every other afternoon we went for a run.

It had been almost a year since my stroke and I had made significant advances both personally and professionally. I had been busy, but that was my choice, and my time was well spent.

A year ago, when I was first recovering from the stroke, I had certainly not imagined that today I would be executive director of a non-profit organization, but that was exactly what I was. I ran everything virtually from my office at home. When I began building the Stroke Support Foundation, I first approached people I knew would be essential to its success.

First and foremost, I was able to hook Dr. Stern on the idea of the program, I enticed her with the prospect of building a large database of individuals that would provide her with the ability to research numerous variables of an individual's progress. For example, she could track and examine strokes in relation to variables such as region, sex, race, income, time to care etc. and also their progress post-stroke.

Though my goal, of course, was initially just to help people, Dr. Stern's group quickly introduced me to the field of health research. I had to get up to speed on topics like epidemiological and multi-variant analysis, and I was required to clearly understand that correlation does not equal causation. After I read up a bit on these types of topics, I never looked at infomercials or product claims the same way again—it was like getting a graduate ducation. And apparently that was good for my brain for my recovery too. Needless to say, there was a lot I ot know about conducting clinical research, a lot.

But my goal really was not to conduct research, it was to increase the accessibly of information and provide access to proven stroke recovery strategies to people who needed them. And I can tell you that after the first five weeks of my own program I really felt like I was just about back to 100%. In fact, I think I had started to feel better than I had in the years leading up to my stroke. Because of my time off I was able to keep a close watch on my health, including how and what I was eating, exercising more regularly, and also exercising the organ I injured—my brain. The program had been a godsend and I was convinced even more than before that I needed to get this program out to the masses.

I continued to train with Thomas, and I asked Thomas and Ella if they would be interested in helping out with the Stroke Support Foundation; their answer was an emphatic yes! So Thomas and Ella joined the organization's board and had been valuable assets to the organization, helping us reach our demographic, guiding the types of messages that were sent out, and advising on how to genuinely connect with people. Thomas had also been a great ambassador of the program, giving talks at different events, which had been great since it turns out he's an excellent public speaker. These two had been a driving force in fundraising for the foundation and in providing general awareness of stroke and stroke recovery.

The Stroke Support Foundation website had been up and running for just over six months. We were able to receive some start-up funding, which had apparently come very quickly according to Dr. Stern—most projects do not receive funding right away. She had explained that unless there was a proof of concept, funds were not normally awarded.

That was baffling to me. To prove a concept you needed money to set the project up. Dr. Stern didn't disagree and simply replied, "Welcome to government funding." I knew we also needed to focus on private funding avenues to ensure we could keep the program rolling.

With the initial funding in place, I was able to piggyback on Dr. Stern's program and use some of her computer programming help from the university to assist with set-up. Leia was right; there was a lot more to starting a website than just setting things up to go online. Some website-building programs include tabs, blogs, and more, but any special programming requires someone to write the code, whatever that is. I just knew how I wanted it to work and to look in the end, and that's what they did: make it work and look right.

I was able to get access to lectures related to stroke and those videos were just a click away on our site, accessible twenty-four hours a day. We could track when and from where the site was accessed via analytics. We created a professional access area on the site for researchers to share advances in research and for questions related to programming. We also added a testimonial section (though I now knew that wasn't the best scientific approach to research) with inspiring stories, both written and on video, to help our participants. This section was heavily used and I think a great asset.

In addition to the blog we had a private forum area where participant questions could be answered privately. Confidentiality was especially important because some individuals don't want to post their questions on the main public site. This function was becoming a lot of work for just me, though, and I was sure that soon I would need help. I had received some very heart-breaking emails, I must say, but the messages about the program changing people's lives had been phenomenal and encouraged me to keep grinding on. I'd printed some of those messages and had them taped on my office wall. It seemed so obvious that an accessible system was badly needed for so many people.

We'd only been up and active for six months but the research world is a very tight-knit community and we'd blasted out emails to hospital programs across the continent, and they'd been very supportive. Many hospitals and rehab facilities in areas that couldn't access this type of system or information locally were now using the program on their own. For example, areas that didn't have support programs for stroke patients had been creating programs and supplementing them with our videos, our online gaming programs, and general one-to-one interactions as advised by our researchers. Not all hospital centers had specialized support staff, but now they didn't need them because everything in the program was laid out for them. The initial feedback from these hospitals indicated that the program was becoming their standard treatment for people who had had strokes.

We had also heard that individuals who had experienced traumatic brain injuries had been engaging in a modified version of the program to assist in their recovery. With all the data coming in from these satellite sites, Dr. Stern was trying to expand her grad student staff and was developing further grant proposals to study all the data.

Our organization was acting as a hub for hospitals and individuals who wanted to know as much as they could. We had been providing tablets through access to technology programs for those who needed them. We had daily messages programmed to be sent to users once they started the program, providing inspiration and reminding them to track their daily exercise, sleep, calories, and so on. If they had signed up for it, we could remotely track their time on task for any of the activities they engage in. We also had occasional testing programs that vary in content but that all test the individual on how they're progressing in certain cognitive areas. This function provides feedback on which areas they need to focus on. This type of specialized programming had, of course, eaten up a significant amount of the budget, and it had been possible to get it all up and running only with Dr. Stern's programming support. But it had been a valuable asset to the program and a learning tool for many of her students.

Later on, I wanted to have our programmers develop a virtual brain showing the areas most likely to be activated during certain tasks. Perhaps we could also develop a system that could track brain activation potentials—essentially electrical output—in real time as people were working on their programs. Individuals would be encouraged to take different cognitive assessments, and our virtual brains would show on-screen changes in brain activation as the patient worked on the various tasks in the assessment, allowing them to see and understand how and why this type of cognitive work was so important for recovery. I believed it would give people hope and help them want to work harder on affected areas or less-active areas of their brains. The little research I had seen on biofeedback showed that it could be highly beneficial.

Every day when I wake up now I have so many things on my plate. Our brain training programs are showing they can bring about change for individuals: we're seeing distinct, measurable progression, sometimes even on a daily basis. It's been an extensive undertaking but the nobility of the task makes every minute I spend on this program worthwhile. My goal is to have the program continue expanding, and ultimately I want to get it to the point where once I leave, we'll be able to hire an excellent executive director to step into the role and keep the ball rolling. We hope to be able to do that over the next year and a half, with government and private funding.

I would stay on the board as an advisor, but for the organization to evolve I would need more expertise. Leia, of course, thinks I'm crazy, working so hard on this every day since I officially retired from the police force. She figured I might slow down a bit but in fact I have done quite the opposite.

I do make time for fun, though. Once in a while I join Thomas and Ella for coffee, for example. They have an extensive group of knowledgeable friends, and the coffee conversation is always exceptional. I have been exercising much more regularly, and I'm down about fifteen pounds. I feel like I keep getting fitter. I got my vision back to where it needs to be—I have just a tiny spot still missing, but nothing that affects my driving. Dr. White was able to allow me to keep my license, so Abigale and I are able to take great car rides with the windows down (well, hers anyway). I splurged a little, okay a lot, when I got a new car—a Shelby Mustang GT350, which puts out 529 horsepower. It's awesome! I'll have to go to pet Wal-Mart and get Abigale a seatbelt harness for long trips. I was pretty sure they'd have them.

As for my to-do list, I've accomplished just about every goal, except for finding a soulmate. Or a sole mate. I did find a great pair running shoes so maybe I reached th goal too. Maybe I'll be perpetually single, with scatte dates here and there to keep me in the game. I guess working on *me* was more important, so maybe finding a mate was a task that needed to happen last anyway. Maybe that's why I put it on the bottom of my list.

I think because I joined the force so young, I didn't have time to find out who I really was, and if I didn't know who I was, how could the person I eventually marry know who they were getting? That might be why so many cops end up divorced, that, and the long hours sometimes for days as well as, often not being at home. And sometimes we have trouble relating to civilians doing jobs that aren't life and death every day. For me, though, I feel like I'm in a good place right now, and wow, it only took me until I retired to get here.

I'm sure that when I'm ready I will run into the right person. I'm sure she's out there. I dream of her once in a while. She has a great smile, long brown hair with a few highlights, and an intense personality that likes to challenge me. She likes to swim, run, walk, and roller-blade. She is responsible and has a kind heart and her weakness is that she cares too much about everything. She would have to be ticklish everywhere and loves dogs. I think that's the woman for me. A guy can dream. When I find the woman of my dreams, I'm going to win her heart.

One of my most important accomplishments has been the endorsement the foundation received from Dr. White. She's a much-sought-after speaker who travels the world presenting at important events, and since she's been on board with the program, we've received a significant amount of exposure. As a result, we've garnered lots of international attention and requests for consultations related to our program and its implementation.

I keep on my desktop a copy of an email Dr. White sent me. When the days get long or I'm in need of some inspiration, I sometimes open it and read it again:

Dear Detective Myles,

It is about 1:00 am and I'm just wrapping up for the day, but before I do, I wanted to let you know I reviewed some of the results Dr. Stern sent along to me in regards to your program. I must admit that at first, I was a little apprehensive about her teaming up with someone with little research experience in this field, but after looking at your recent results I can most certainly say the contribution you have made to this program exceeds all my expectations, which I assure you is very difficult to do. The simplicity of your approach, just getting in the trenches and helping people that need help, is sometimes lost on researchers, as our focus is spread across a lot of areas, including the logistics involved in such a program, so we truly cannot see the forest for the trees sometimes.

Though I have been working in this field for several decades and I have done my utmost to help as many people as I can, I can see in your results, and in your program numbers to date, how many lives you have already affected and I commend you for that. You have my admiration and support and should you or Dr. Stern need assistance with lobbying the hospital for further resources or additional access, I will be happy to help. As well, if either of you need a partner on any aspects of your program, I will be there to lend a hand.

Finally, I want to say thank you, Detective Myles, for all your hard work, your vision, and your willingness to make a difference when it counts the most. I'm sure you will com to see in the very near future what a difference you ha made for so many individuals.

Sometimes a star (like you) just needs a chance to shine and the ones that seize the moment turn out to be the brightest stars in the sky.

All the best from one of your fans. Shine on!!

Evelyn

REFERENCES

1. "The Knowledge," The London Taxi Experience. www.the-london-taxi.com.

2. E.A. Maguire, D.G. Gadian, I.S. Johnsrude, C.D. Good, J. Ashburner, R.S.J. Frackowiak, and C.D. Frith, "Navigation-Related Structural Change in the Hippocampi of Taxi Drivers," *Proceedings of the National Academy of Sciences of the United States of America* 97 (Apr. 11, 2000): 4398–4403. http://www.pnas.org/cgi/doi/10.1073/pnas.070039597.

3. L.S. Williams, E.Y. Yilmaz, and A.M. Lopez-Yunez, "Retrospective Assessment of Initial Stroke Severity with the NIH Stroke Scale," *Stroke* 31 (Apr. 2000): 858–862. http://www.ncbi.nlm.nih.gov/pubmed/12865618.

4. D. Schlegel, S.J. Kolb, J.M. Luciano, J.M. Tovar, B.L. Cucchiara, D.S. Liebeskind, and S.E. Kasner, "Utility of the NIH Stroke Scale as a Predictor of Hospital Disposition," *Stroke* 34 (Jan. 2003): 134–137. https://www.ncbi.nlm.nih.gov/pubmed/12511764.

5. G.W. Albers, L.R. Caplan, J.D. Easton, P.B. Fayad, J.P. Mohr, J.L. Saver, and D.G. Sherman for the TIA Working Group, "Transient Ischemic Attack—Proposal for a New Definition," *New England Journal of Medicine* 347 (Nov. 21, 2002): 1713–1716. https://www.nejm.org/doi/full/10.1056/NEJMsb020987.

6. S.R. Messé and E.C. Jauch, "Transient Ischemic Attack: Diagnostic Evaluation." *Annals of Emergency Medicine* 52 (Aug. 2008): S17–26. https://www.annemergmed.com/article/S0196-0644(08)00833-0/abstract.

7. American Stroke Association. "Stroke Risk Factors." https://www.strokeassociation.org/en/about-stroke/stroke-risk-factors.

8. National Center for Chronic Disease Prevention and Health Promotion (US) Office on Smoking and Health, *The Health Consequences of Smoking—50 Years of Progress: A Report of the Surgeon General* (Atlanta, GA: Centers for Disease Control and Prevention, 2014). https://www.ncbi.nlm.nih.gov/books/NBK179276/.

9. I.J. Brown, I. Tzoulaki, V. Candeias, and P. Elliott, "Salt Intakes Around the World: Implications for Public Health," *International Journal of Epidemiology* 38 (June 2009): 791–813. http://ije.oxfordjournals.org/content/early/2009/04/07/ije.d yp139.full.

10. P. Strazzullo, L. D'Elia, N.-B. Kandala, and F.P. Cappuccio, "Salt Intake, Stroke, and Cardiovascular Disease: Meta-Analysis of Prospective Studies," *BMJ* 339 (Nov. 25, 2009): b4567. http://www.bmj.com/content/339/bmj.b4567.full.

11. V.L. Roger, A.S. Go, D.M. Lloyd-Jones, R.J. Adams, J.D. Berry, T.M. Brown, M.R. Carnethon, et al., "Heart Disease and Stroke Statistics—2011 Update: A Report from the American Heart Association," *Circulation* 123 (Feb. 1, 2011): e18–e209. http://circ.ahajournals.org/content/123/4/e18.full.

12. B. Thanvi and T. Robinson, "Complete Occlusion of Extracranial Internal Carotid Artery: Clinical Features, Pathophysiology, Diagnosis and Management," *Postgraduate Medical Journal* 83 (2007): 95–99. http://www.ncbi.nlm.nih.gov/pmc/articles/PMC2805948/pdf /95.pdf.

13. J.M. Wardlaw, V. Murray, E. Berge, and G.J. del Zoppo, "Thrombolysis for Acute Ischaemic Stroke," *Cochrane Database of Systematic Reviews* 7 (2014). http://www.ncbi.nlm.nih.gov/pmc/articles/PMC4153726/pdf /nihms618736.pdf

14. Q. Ma, C. Chu, and H. Song, "Intravenous versus Intra-arterial Thrombolysis in Ischemic Stroke: A Systematic Review and Meta-analysis," *PLoS One* 10 (Jan. 8, 2015): e0116120. http://www.pubmedcentral.nih.gov/articlerender.fcgi?artid=4 287629&tool=pmcentrez&rendertype=abstract.

15. T. Kurth, J.M. Gaziano, and K. Berger, "Body Mass Index and the Risk of Stroke in Men," *Archives of Internal Medicine* 162 (Dec. 9, 2002): 2557–2562. https://jamanetwork.com/journals/jamainternalmedicine/full article/754810.

16. R.D. Abbott, G.R. Behrens, D.S. Sharp, B.L. Rodriguez, C.M. Burchfiel, G.W. Ross, K. Yano, and J.D. Curb, "Body Mass Index and Thromboembolic Stroke in Nonsmoking Men in Older Middle Age. The Honolulu Heart Program," *Stroke* 25 (Dec. 1994): 2370–2376. https://www.ncbi.nlm.nih.gov/pubmed/7974575.

17. K. Jood, C. Jern, L. Wilhelmsen, and A. Rosengren, "Body Mass Index in Mid-life Is Associated with a First Stroke in Men: A Prospective Population Study over 28 Years," *Stroke* 35 (Dec. 1, 2004): 2764–2769. https://www.ahajournals.org/doi/full/10.1161/01.STR.00001 47715.58886.ad.

18. Y.-M. Song, J. Sung, G.D. Smith, and S. Ebrahim, "Body Mass Index and Ischemic and Hemorrhagic Stroke: A Prospective Study in Korean Men," *Stroke* 35 (Apr. 1, 2004): 831–836. https://www.ahajournals.org/doi/10.1161/01.str.000011938 6.22691.1c.

19. A. Barbarossa, F. Guerra, and A. Capucci, "Silent Atrial Fibrillation: A Critical Review," *Journal of Atrial Fibrillation* 7 (Oct. 31, 2014): 39–44. https://www.ncbi.nlm.nih.gov/pmc/articles/PMC4956292/.

20. W.S. Aronow and M. Banach, "Atrial Fibrillation: The New Epidemic of the Ageing World," *Journal of Atrial Fibrillation* 1 (Apr. 1, 2009): 337–361. https://www.ncbi.nlm.nih.gov/pmc/articles/PMC5398780/.

21. B.M. Collins, and H.J. Stam, "A Transnational Perspective on Psychosurgery: Beyond Portugal and the United States," *Journal of the History of the Neurosciences* 23 (2014): 335–354. https://www.ncbi.nlm.nih.gov/pubmed/25116422.

22. Canadian Institute for Health Information, *All-Cause Readmission to Acute Care and Return to the Emergency Department* (Ottawa, ON: CIHI, 2012). https://secure.cihi.ca/free_products/Readmission_to_acutecar e_en.pdf.

23. C. Pellegrini, "Canada Ranks Low on Patient Safety in International Comparison," *CMAJ* 186 (Jan. 7, 2014): E12. http://www.cmaj.ca/content/186/1/E12.

24. M.F.K. Suri and A.I. Qureshi, "Readmission within 1 Month of Discharge Among Patients with Acute Ischemic Stroke: Results of the University HealthSystem Consortium Stroke Benchmarking Study," *Journal of Vascular and Interventional Neurology* 6 (Dec. 2013): 47–51. https://www.ncbi.nlm.nih.gov/pmc/articles/PMC3868247/?t ool=pmcentrez&report=abstract.

25. William J. Tippett, *Building an Ageless Mind: Preventing and Fighting Brain Aging and Disease* (Lanham, MD: Rowman & Littlefield, 2013).

26. Brain Aneurysm Foundation. "About Brain Aneurysms." Cited June 8, 2016. http://www.bafound.org.

27. A. Wong and S.J. Read, "Early Changes in Physiological Variables after Stroke," *Annals of Indian Academy of Neurology* 11 (Oct.–Dec. 2008): 207–220. https://www.ncbi.nlm.nih.gov/pmc/articles/PMC2771993/.

28. R.J. Seitz and G.A. Donnan, "Recovery Potential after Acute Stroke," *Frontiers in Neurology* 6 (Nov. 11, 2015). https://www.frontiersin.org/articles/10.3389/fneur.2015.002 38/full.

ACKNOWLEDGMENTS

Heart and Stroke Foundation Centre for Stroke Recovery

CPSIA information can be obtained
at www.ICGtesting.com
Printed in the USA
LVHW111919120220
646719LV00005B/887